Pastors & Patriots

Pastors & Patriots

The Muhlenberg Family of Pennsylvania

This catalogue is a special edition of *Der Reggeboge*

Journal of the Pennsylvania German Society

Volume 45 • **2011** • Number 1

© 2011 The Philip and Muriel Berman Museum of Art at Ursinus College

The Berman Museum of Art gratefully acknowledges the Shelley Pennsylvania German Heritage Fund for its generous support of this publication and the accompanying exhibition.

Pastors & Patriots: The Muhlenberg Family of Pennsylvania has been selected by the Pennsylvania German Society as volume 45, number 1, of *Der Reggeboge*, the journal of the Pennsylvania German Society.

ISBN: 978-1-889136-23-3

Editors: Onie Rollins and Thomas J. Gerhart

Copy Editor: Carolyn C. Wenger

Principal photographer: Glenn Holcombe

Designer: Jennifer Glosser, 2 Pug Design, Jonestown, Pa.

Front cover: Detail of winged angel head from St. Luke Lutheran Church, Schaefferstown, Lebanon County, c. 1767 (fig. 1.31). Collection of Katharine and Robert Booth

Back cover: Pair of pistols owned by Peter Muhlenberg, England, c. 1770–75 (fig. 2.12). American Revolution Center

Half-title page *(left to right)*: Portrait miniatures of Peter Muhlenberg and Henry Melchior Muhlenberg, probably Pennsylvania, c. 1785 (figs. 2.14 and 3.4). Collection of a descendant

CONTENTS

Foreword vii

Acknowledgments ix

Introduction 1

CHAPTER ONE
Pastors 7

CHAPTER TWO
Patriots 35

CHAPTER THREE
Patriarchs 49

APPENDIX A
Gallery of Missing, Unidentified, and Miscellaneous Objects 73

APPENDIX B
The First Three Generations of the Muhlenberg Family 85

Endnotes 87

FOREWORD

The Philip and Muriel Berman Museum of Art is situated on the campus of Ursinus College, founded in 1869 and deeply rooted in Pennsylvania German history. The college is little more than a mile from the restored home of Henry Melchior Muhlenberg and the nearby residence of his son Frederick Augustus Muhlenberg, now called the Speaker's House, which functioned as a dormitory for the college (known as Highland Hall) from 1924 to 1944.

With a long-standing interest in Pennsylvania German culture and as home to the Pennsylvania Folklife Society collection, the Berman Museum hosted an exhibition in 1992 to commemorate the 250th anniversary of the arrival of Henry Melchior Muhlenberg in America. Continuing that tradition, this publication and the accompanying exhibition at the museum not only mark the 300th anniversary of Muhlenberg's birth, September 6, 1711, but also celebrate the Muhlenberg family's considerable contributions to American history and culture. In a larger sense, they make an important contribution to our understanding of the Pennsylvania German and provide a groundbreaking look at the material culture associated with elite families such as the Muhlenbergs.

We are pleased to present *Pastors & Patriots*, which honors the Berman Museum's ongoing commitment to highlighting the richness of our local history, the Muhlenberg family, and our Pennsylvania German heritage.

LISA TREMPER HANOVER
Director, Philip and Muriel Berman Museum of Art at Ursinus College

ACKNOWLEDGMENTS

This catalogue is the culmination of an eight-year journey that began in 2003 when I was a student at Ursinus College. Working under Dr. Dallett Hemphill, I wrote a research paper on the Muhlenbergs for a course on the history of the family. That project led me to discover the journals and papers of Henry Melchior Muhlenberg and whetted my appetite to study further those rich primary sources. More involvement came with my organization of a loan exhibition from the Pennsylvania German collection of the Berman Museum of Art that was installed at the Henry Muhlenberg House in Trappe. I continued to research the Muhlenbergs during my senior year and completed a 250-page study of the family for my history thesis. To pursue a distinguished honors degree, I was required to have an outside reader for the thesis, which led me to Dr. A. Gregg Roeber, a professor at the Pennsylvania State University and a scholar of German Lutherans in colonial Pennsylvania. During that time I also learned of efforts to rescue the Trappe home of Frederick Muhlenberg from demolition and soon became involved there as well.

After graduation from Ursinus in 2006, I pursued a master's degree in the Winterthur Program in Early American Culture, where my interest in the Muhlenbergs and a newfound love of architecture from working with Dr. Bernie Herman culminated in a master's thesis on the Muhlenberg family houses in Trappe. For the next several years I continued to research, study, write, and lecture on the Muhlenbergs while also working on a major exhibition and catalogue of southeastern Pennsylvania furniture at Winterthur. The 300th anniversary of Henry Melchior Muhlenberg's birth, September 6, 1711, then provided the impetus to organize an exhibition on the family and write the accompanying catalogue.

A project of this duration and scope could not have been possible without the kind and generous assistance of many individuals and foundations, in particular the Shelley Pennsylvania German Heritage Fund, which provided financial support for the exhibition and catalogue. I am also deeply indebted to those who shared their collections and assisted during the documentation, research, writing, conservation, and photography phases of this study, including Alan Andersen, Kory Berrett, Robert and Kathy Booth, Philip Bradley, William K. du Pont, Mike Emery, Lou Farrell, Lydia Garver, Jim Gergat and Kathy Lesieur, Pat Gibble, Alyce Graham, Andrew Grasberger, Alan Gutchess, Mike Hart, Steve Hench, Brian and Barbara Hendelson, Chip Henderson, Don Herr, Glenn Holcombe, Alan Keyser, Jim Lewars, Deirdre Pook Magarelli, Ron and James Pook, Chris Rebollo, Lynn Roberts, Elle Shushan, John J. Snyder Jr., Don Tharpe, Glenys Waldman, the late Pastor Frederick S. Weiser, Hermann Wellenreuther, Barbara Wentz, and Jean Woods.

One of the greatest pleasures of this project has been getting to know many of the current generations of Muhlenberg descendants who kindly assisted in my research, including Douglas and Diane Blake, Elizabeth Muhlenberg Brooke Blake, Lindsay Clinton, Jeremy Cooper, Martha Muhlenberg Doto, Greta Wagner Fiest, Peter and Bonnie Goetz, Taylor, Pippa, and Henley Goetz, Sarah Muhlenberg Grace, Walter Hiester, Caroline Muhlenberg Hufford-Anderson, Nancy Lawson, Joan and Gordon Lehman, Suzanne Wagner Magee, Cathy Millard, Caroline Hiester Mills, the late Dr. John Peter Gabriel Muhlenberg, David Muhlenberg, Jerome Muhlenberg, John A. Muhlenberg, John D. S. Muhlenberg, Mimi and Sarah Muhlenberg, Sven and Jessica Muhlenberg, Ted and Kitty Stokes, Ted Stokes, Chad Wagner, Tim Wagner, the late Tom Wagner, and William Muhlenberg Wagner Jr.

Colleagues and friends at numerous churches, historical societies, museums, and libraries were also essential to the success of this project, including: American Revolution Center, Scott Stephenson; American Philosophical Society, Valerie-Ann Lutz; Augustus Lutheran Church, Dick Buckmaster, Karen McClain, Rev. Herbert H. Michel, Rev. G. Warren Weleck Jr.; Bartram's Garden, Joel Fry; Colonial Williamsburg Foundation, Linda Baumgarten, Virginia Foster, Barbara Luck, Ken Schwarz, John Watson, Carolyn Weekley; Conrad Weiser Homestead; Diplomatic Reception Rooms, U.S. Department of State, Marcee Craighill; Francke Foundations, Jürgen Gröschl, Dorothea Hornemann, Thomas Müller-Bahlke, Claus Veltmann; Franklin and Marshall College, Claire Giblin, Michael Lear; Free Library of Philadelphia, Janine Pollock, Joseph Shemtov; Historic Schaefferstown, Inc., Diane Wenger; Historical Society of Berks County, Joshua Blay; Historical Society of Montgomery County, Jeff McGranahan; Historical Society of Trappe, Collegeville, Perkiomen Valley, Bridgie Daller, Dona McDermott, Rev. Bob Meschke, Linda Wiernusz; Lutheran Theological Seminary at Philadelphia, Rev. Dr. Karl Krueger, Natalie Hand, John Peterson, Mary Redline; Muhlenberg College, Kathy Burke, Diane Koch, Rev. Peter Bredlau; Lancaster County Historical Society, Marianne Heckles, Barry Rauhauser, Tom Ryan, Robin Sarratt; Library Company of Philadelphia, Nicole Joniec, Sarah Weatherwax; Moravian Archives, Lanie Graf; National Portrait Gallery, Brandon Brame Fortune, Lizanne Reger; New Hanover Lutheran Church, Lee Wesner; New-York Historical Society, Nicole Contaxis, Margi Hofer; Preservation Society of Newport County, Paul Miller, Miranda Peters; Pennsylvania State University, A. Gregg Roeber; Pennsylvania State University Libraries, Sandy Stelts; Pennypacker Mills, Carl Klase; Trinity Lutheran Church, Lancaster, Andrea Collins, Joan Kahler; and Ursinus College, Peter Luborsky, Carolyn Weigel, John Wickersham. A special note of thanks is due to my colleagues at Winterthur Museum, in particular, Onie Rollins for editing the manuscript. Curators Wendy

Cooper, Linda Eaton, Don Fennimore, Leslie Grigsby, and Ann Wagner provided input on various objects; Jennifer Mass assisted with scientific analysis; Jim Schneck and Laszlo Bodo took some of the photographs, as coordinated by Susan Newton; Emily Guthrie, Helena Richardson, and Jeanne Solensky assisted with library research; and Felice Lamden, Amy Marks Delaney, and Nat Caccamo advised me on the exhibition installation.

I especially thank the Pennsylvania German Society, in particular editors Thomas J. Gerhart and Carolyn C. Wenger, for their collaboration in selecting this catalogue as a special edition of *Der Reggeboge*. I also gratefully acknowledge the staff of the Berman Museum of Art for hosting the exhibition and helping to coordinate the countless details that arise with such an endeavor, including director Lisa Tremper Hanover and museum staff Sue Calvin, Julie Choma, and Susan Shifrin. In addition, I thank the members of the Historic Muhlenberg Partnership, a collaborative effort of Augustus Lutheran Church, the Borough of Trappe, Historical Society of Trappe, Collegeville, Perkiomen Valley, Inc., and the Speaker's House, who provided significant support, including those named elsewhere as well as Russ Henze, Ed Hiergesell, Dea Mingis, Connie Peck, and Fred Schuetz.

Special recognition is due to several mentors who sadly passed away before this project was completed. The late Dr. John Peter Gabriel Muhlenberg was for many years the family historian and provided strong encouragement in the early stages of my research, while the late Pastor Frederick S. Weiser, longtime secretary of the Weiser Family Association, helped me make contact with numerous Muhlenberg descendants. The late Dr. John C. Shetler, former historian of the Historical Society of Trappe, worked with me on the loan exhibition at the Henry Muhlenberg House in 2003. All three men shared their love and knowledge of the Muhlenberg family and were greatly influential in my continuing pursuit of this research.

Finally, to my family and friends who have endured my study of all things Muhlenberg for the past eight years, a heartfelt note of thanks for your love and support, in particular to my mother, Kate Minardi, who assisted with countless hours of archival research and helped shed light on many details of historic Trappe and the Muhlenberg family. I know they will understand that this publication is only the tip of the iceberg and that the subject will continue to be an ongoing passion for many years to come.

LISA MINARDI
Guest curator, *Pastors & Patriots*
President, The Speaker's House, Home of Frederick Muhlenberg

FIGURE 1
The Orphanage at Glaucha near Halle and *Southern Prospect of the Orphanage and School Buildings*, engraved by Gottfried August Gründler, 1749. Francke Foundations

INTRODUCTION

Born on September 6, 1711, Henry Melchior Muhlenberg was the son of Nicolaus Melchior Muhlenberg, a shoemaker, and Anna Maria Kleinschmidt, daughter of a Prussian military officer (figs. 1 and 2).[1] The family lived in the town of Einbeck, located in the electorate of Hannover, now in north-central Germany (fig. 3). A Lutheran stronghold, Einbeck had suffered during the Thirty Years' War but was rebuilt in 1718 by King George II of England, who was also the electoral prince of Hannover. At the age of seven, Henry was sent to a classical school, where he received instruction in Latin. Five years later he was confirmed in the Lutheran Church. His father's death in 1729 led to a hiatus in young Henry's education as he was obligated to help support the family through manual labor.

FIGURE 2
Portrait of Henry Melchior Muhlenberg (1711–87), probably after Jacob Eichholtz (1776–1842), Pennsylvania, c. 1825–50. Oil on canvas. Preservation Society of Newport County, gift of Mrs. Alletta Morris McBean

FIGURE 3
Map of Germany showing the locations of Einbeck, Göttingen, and Halle. Tom Willcockson, Mapcraft.com

FIGURE 4
Orphanage at Halle, built 1698–1701. Francke Foundations, photo by Ingo Gottlieb

FIGURE 5
Portrait of August Hermann Francke (1663–1727), c. 1725. Oil on canvas. Francke Foundations

Several patrons took notice of the young man, including Dr. Joachim Oporin, professor of theology at the University of Göttingen (founded in 1734 by George II), which Muhlenberg entered in 1735. There he studied Greek, Hebrew, mathematics, logic, and theology and received a broad understanding of Christian history that would later stand him in good stead when confronted with colonial Pennsylvania's religious pluralism. He then went to the Francke Institutions (fig. 4) in Halle, a renowned center of education and philanthropy founded in 1695 by August Hermann Francke (fig. 5).[2] Muhlenberg taught in the orphanage school there and became an inspector of the infirmary. Halle was also a center of Pietism, an evangelical movement of religious and social reform that would deeply influence Muhlenberg's views on spirituality and moral behavior. On August 24, 1739, he was ordained a Lutheran minister (fig. 6) and served a congregation in Grosshennersdorf. Henry thought of going to India as a missionary but on his thirtieth birth-

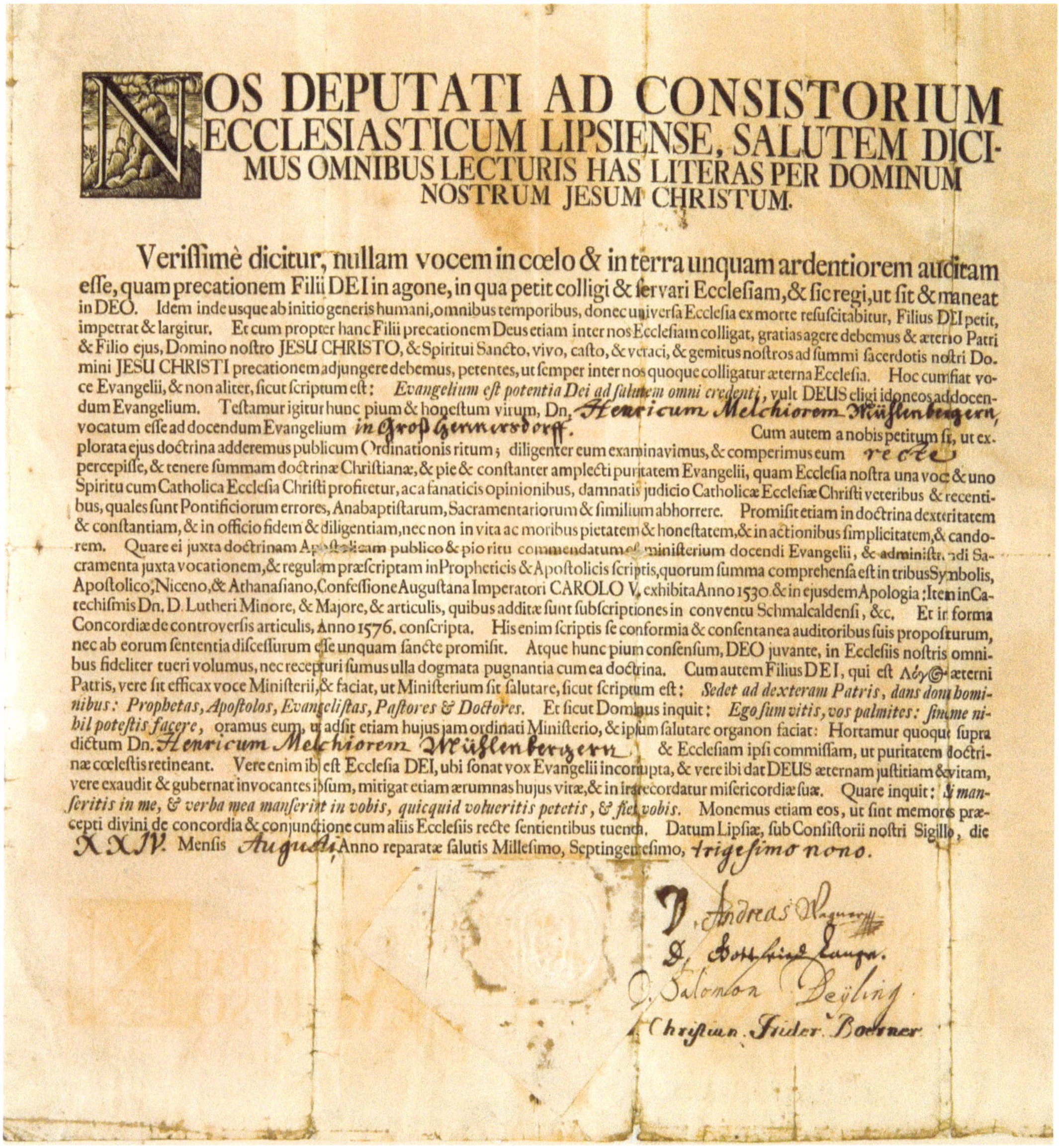
NOS DEPUTATI AD CONSISTORIUM ECCLESIASTICUM LIPSIENSE, SALUTEM DICIMUS OMNIBUS LECTURIS HAS LITERAS PER DOMINUM NOSTRUM JESUM CHRISTUM.

Verissimè dicitur, nullam vocem in cœlo & in terra unquam ardentiorem auditam esse, quam precationem Filii DEI in agone, in qua petit colligi & servari Ecclesiam, & sic regi, ut sit & maneat in DEO. Idem inde usque ab initio generis humani, omnibus temporibus, donec universa Ecclesia ex morte resuscitabitur, Filius DEI petit, impetrat & largitur. Et cum propter hanc Filii precationem Deus etiam inter nos Ecclesiam colligat, gratias agere debemus & æterno Patri & Filio ejus, Domino nostro JESU CHRISTO, & Spiritui Sancto, vivo, casto, & veraci, & gemitus nostros ad summi sacerdotis nostri Domini JESU CHRISTI precationem adjungere debemus, petentes, ut semper inter nos quoque colligatur æterna Ecclesia. Hoc cum fiat voce Evangelii, & non aliter, sicut scriptum est: *Evangelium est potentia Dei ad salutem omni credenti*, vult DEUS eligi idoneos ad docendum Evangelium. Testamur igitur hunc pium & honestum virum, Dn. Henricum Melchiorem Mühlenbergern, vocatum esse ad docendum Evangelium in Groß Hennersdorff. Cum autem a nobis petitum sit, ut explorata ejus doctrina adderemus publicum Ordinationis ritum; diligenter eum examinavimus, & comperimus eum recte percepisse, & tenere summam doctrinæ Christianæ, & pie & constanter amplecti puritatem Evangelii, quam Ecclesia nostra una voce & uno Spiritu cum Catholica Ecclesia Christi profitetur, ac a fanaticis opinionibus, damnatis judicio Catholicæ Ecclesiæ Christi veteribus & recentibus, quales sunt Pontificiorum errores, Anabaptistarum, Sacramentariorum & similium abhorrere. Promisit etiam in doctrina dexteritatem & constantiam, & in officio fidem & diligentiam, nec non in vita ac moribus pietatem & honestatem, & in actionibus simplicitatem, & candorem. Quare ei juxta doctrinam Apostolicam publico & pio ritu commendatum est ministerium docendi Evangelii, & administrandi Sacramenta juxta vocationem, & regulam præscriptam in Propheticis & Apostolicis scriptis, quorum summa comprehensa est in tribus Symbolis, Apostolico, Niceno, & Athanasiano, Confessione Augustana Imperatori CAROLO V. exhibita Anno 1530. & in ejusdem Apologia; Item in Catechismis Dn. D. Lutheri Minore, & Majore, & articulis, quibus additæ sunt subscriptiones in conventu Schmalcaldensi, &c. Et in forma Concordiæ de controversis articulis, Anno 1576. conscripta. His enim scriptis se conformia & consentanea auditoribus suis propositurum, nec ab eorum sententia discessurum esse unquam sancte promisit. Atque hunc pium consensum, DEO juvante, in Ecclesiis nostris omnibus fideliter tueri volumus, nec recepturi sumus ulla dogmata pugnantia cum ea doctrina. Cum autem Filius DEI, qui est Λόγος æterni Patris, vere sit efficax voce Ministerii, & faciat, ut Ministerium sit salutare, sicut scriptum est: *Sedet ad dexteram Patris, dans dona hominibus: Prophetas, Apostolos, Evangelistas, Pastores & Doctores.* Et sicut Dominus inquit: *Ego sum vitis, vos palmites: sine me nihil potestis facere*, oramus eum, ut adsit etiam hujus jam ordinati Ministerio, & ipsum salutare organon faciat: Hortamur quoque supra dictum Dn. Henricum Melchiorem Mühlenbergern, & Ecclesiam ipsi commissam, ut puritatem doctrinæ cœlestis retineant. Vere enim ibi est Ecclesia DEI, ubi sonat vox Evangelii incorrupta, & vere ibi dat DEUS æternam justitiam & vitam, vere exaudit & gubernat invocantes ipsum, mitigat etiam ærumnas hujus vitæ, & in ira recordatur misericordiæ suæ. Quare inquit: *Si manseritis in me, & verba mea manserint in vobis, quicquid volueritis petetis, & fiet vobis.* Monemus etiam eos, ut sint memores præcepti divini de concordia & conjunctione cum aliis Ecclesiis recte sentientibus tuenda. Datum Lipsiæ, sub Consistorii nostri Sigillo, die XXIV. Mensis Augusti, Anno reparatæ salutis Millesimo, Septingentesimo, trigesimo nono.

D. Andreas Wagner

D. Gottfried Lange

D. Salomon Deyling

Christian Friedr. Börner

FIGURE 6
Certificate of ordination of Henry Melchior Muhlenberg, dated August 24, 1739. Lutheran Archives Center, Lutheran Theological Seminary at Philadelphia

day, September 6, 1741, was offered a different opportunity. Gotthilf August Francke (fig. 7), who succeeded his father as director of the Halle Institutions, presented Muhlenberg with an appeal from three Lutheran congregations in Pennsylvania that were in dire need of a pastor.

Henry decided to accept the call to Pennsylvania and took leave of his benefactors. He traveled first to Einbeck to say goodbye to his mother and siblings, where he arrived on February 17, 1742, and then made his way to London, where in April he took up lodging near Friedrich Michael Ziegenhagen (fig. 8), the German Lutheran chaplain of the Royal Chapel of Saint James. On May 24, Muhlenberg received the formal call to Pennsylvania and his credentials from Ziegenhagen, who made arrangements for him to visit a settlement of Protestant refugees from Salzburg, Austria, in Ebenezer, Georgia, before going to Philadelphia. On June 13, the ship set sail. The voyage was long and harrowing, compounded by the stormy seas and sinful ways of his fellow passengers. On September 22, the ship finally anchored in Charleston, South Carolina, and Henry offered a prayer of thanksgiving. He then traveled on to Georgia, where he made his way inland via the Savannah

FIGURE 7
Portrait of Gotthilf August Francke (1696–1769), c. 1765. Oil on canvas. Francke Foundations

FIGURE 8
Portrait of Friedrich Michael Ziegenhagen (1694–1776), engraved by G. L. Smith, c. 1770. Francke Foundations

River to Ebenezer. On November 12, he boarded a small sloop that was heading to Philadelphia, where he arrived on November 25 (fig. 9). Having finally reached his destination, Muhlenberg learned that the Philadelphia congregation had disintegrated into factions and the two country congregations of Providence (Trappe) and New Hanover were also falling apart. His work as a pastor had only just begun.

For the next forty-five years, Henry Melchior Muhlenberg worked tirelessly among the German Lutheran settlers. He founded congregations and oversaw the construction of new churches while also leading the Lutheran Ministerium of Pennsylvania and serving as full-time pastor to three congregations—earning him the title patriarch of the Lutheran Church in America. Muhlenberg was also a devoted husband and the father of eleven children, many of whom became famous in their own rights. This is the story of Henry Melchior Muhlenberg, his descendants, and their legacy.

FIGURE 9
The East Prospect of the City of Philadelphia in the Province of Pennsylvania, by George Heap, from the *London Magazine* (1761). American Philosophical Society

FIGURE 1.1
Detail of portrait of Henry Melchior Muhlenberg in fig. 3.10, *Denkmal der Liebe und Achtung . . . dem Herrn Heinrich Melchior Mühlenberg* (Philadelphia: Melchior Steiner, 1788). Lutheran Archives Center, Lutheran Theological Seminary at Philadelphia

CHAPTER ONE
PASTORS

Founded in 1682 by William Penn (1644–1718), Pennsylvania was settled by people with a wide variety of religious views and ethnic backgrounds owing to Penn's policy of religious tolerance. Referred to by Quaker merchant Jonathan Dickinson of Philadelphia in 1717 as a "great mixt multitude," the population of Pennsylvania was the most culturally diverse of the thirteen colonies and included English, Welsh, and Irish Quakers, Scots-Irish Presbyterians, Lutherans, Reformed, Mennonites, Schwenkfelders, Brethren, and countless other religious denominations.[1] The situation of the German Lutheran Church in colonial Pennsylvania was quite different from what Henry Muhlenberg (fig. 1.1) was accustomed to in Germany. He struggled initially to adapt, writing later in 1774, "During the first years a man is blind, so to speak. . . . He misses the ways he is used to and judges the alien conditions by the standards he has brought from the Fatherland."[2] Not only was there no official or established church, but the colonial Pennsylvania government did not interfere in religious affairs, leaving ministers to resolve their own congregational issues. The population was also widely dispersed, with great distances between congregations and few actual churches. During the initial decades of settlement, most immigrants focused on basic survival and could not afford to build churches and schools or pay ministers and schoolmasters. As settlement progressed, wealthier members often assisted in supporting the erection of churches, which tended to encourage congregational rather than pastoral authority and, in some cases, fomented factionalism and disputes.[3] There were also "scoffers" who chose not to attend church at all, leading Lutheran schoolmaster Gottlieb Mittelberger to observe in the 1750s that "Pennsylvania is the heaven of the farmers, the paradise of the mechanics, and the hell of the officials and preachers."[4]

FIGURE 1.2
Portrait of Nicolaus Ludwig von Zinzendorf (1700–1760), attributed to Johann Valentin Haidt (1700–1780), 1747. Oil on canvas. Moravian Archives, Herrnhut GS 045

One of the greatest difficulties Muhlenberg faced was the lack of ordained ministers. Prior to his arrival, various other clergymen (some of them disgraced or unordained) had worked their way into the Lutheran congregations, and Count Nicolaus Ludwig von Zinzendorf (1700–1760), the Moravian leader, had also gained many supporters (fig. 1.2). The majority of the Philadelphia Lutherans had become followers of Zinzendorf while the others had gone over to Johann Valentine Kraft, a recent German émigré who, according to Muhlenberg, led a rather scandalous life. The Trappe congregation had also become attached to Kraft, and the New Hanover congregation was under the influence of a quack doctor named Johann Georg Schmidt. In one of Muhlenberg's first letters to Halle after his arrival in Pennsylvania, he complained, "Here there is no governing authority: elders and deacons are of no account. People do not listen to them but everybody is free and does as he pleases." Thus, he wrote, "A preacher must fight his way through with the sword of the Spirit alone."[5]

Muhlenberg set to work to gain control of the situation. He hired a horse and guide to take

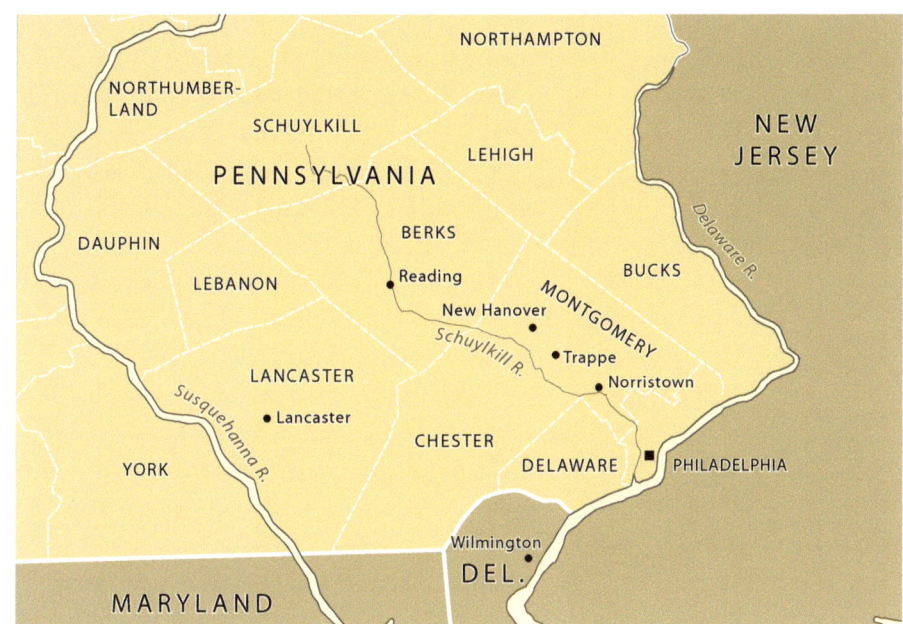

FIGURE 1.3
Map of southeastern Pennsylvania, showing the locations of Philadelphia, New Hanover, and Trappe. Tom Willcockson, Mapcraft.com

him to Trappe and New Hanover, located some thirty miles northwest of Philadelphia (fig. 1.3). On November 28, 1742, he preached his first sermon in Pennsylvania, in New Hanover, where a church "had been built of plain logs, erected about a year before, but not yet finished on the inside."[6] Muhlenberg learned that Pastor Schmidt was not universally popular among the New Hanover congregation because of his scandalous lifestyle and heavy drinking. The next day Muhlenberg went to Providence, or "the Trap" (later Trappe) as the locals called it. The settlement was named after a tavern operated by the Schrack family, who emigrated from Germany and settled there in 1717. Henry met with one of the deacons about the situation and on December 12 delivered his first sermon in Trappe, "in the senior deacon's barn, since the poor people there have no church as yet." After rebuffing Kraft's efforts to assert authority over him, Muhlenberg presented the Trappe congregation with his formal call and letter of support from Court Preacher Friedrich Michael Ziegenhagen. After holding church services in New Hanover on Christmas Day, he met with the deacons and elders of both congregations, who agreed to accept him as their minister. Next he went to Philadelphia, where the non-Zinzendorf faction of the Lutheran congregation also accepted his call. The final hurdle was Zinzendorf himself, a European noble, devout Christian, and ordained Lutheran minister who had become the leader of the Moravian church. The previous year, Zinzendorf had traveled to Pennsylvania to establish the Moravian community of Bethlehem. He hoped to unite the German church people and sectarians into one group, to be known as "The Pennsylvania Congregation of God in the Spirit." Zinzendorf and Muhlenberg met on December 30, 1742, at Zinzendorf's lodging. Although Zinzendorf challenged the legitimacy of Muhlenberg's call, Muhlenberg persevered, insisting that he was following his instructions and that his call had already been accepted by two of the Lutheran congregations.[7]

For the next forty-five years, Muhlenberg devoted himself to the Lutheran Church in America, taking as his motto *Ecclesia plantanda* (the church must be planted). He proved to be a skillful organizer, perhaps because orderliness was next to godliness in his mind. "God is a God of order," he wrote in 1765, "and in His congregations everything must be done orderly."[8] Within months of his arrival, Muhlenberg began building churches and obtaining the proper accoutrements. On January 16, 1743, he lamented the lack of communion vessels: "It is so very difficult for us to obtain a chalice here; there is none who is able or willing to make one, so as yet we do not have one. I might well wish for a pair of them, even if they were only copper or tin."

FIGURE 1.4
Augustus Lutheran Church, built 1743, photo c. 1940, Trappe, Montgomery County. The oldest extant German Lutheran church in Pennsylvania, Augustus has survived in remarkably unaltered condition and is a National Historic Landmark. The exterior stucco is a later addition, first applied in 1814. Augustus Lutheran Church, Trappe, Pa.

FIGURE 1.5
Date stone of Augustus Lutheran Church, 1743.

Because of the number of people who turned out to hear Muhlenberg preach in Trappe, some of the church services had to be moved outside the barn they were using. The congregation began hauling stones to the site, and Muhlenberg noted on January 5 that "already we have erected a schoolhouse of wood." The masons started work on the church by April, and on May 2 the cornerstone was laid. With the roof completed by August 31, the first service was held in the building on September 12 (fig. 1.4). A date stone with Latin inscription above the main entrance bears the name of Henry Melchior Muhlenberg along with names of the founding church wardens: Johann Nicolaus Cressman, Friedrich Marstellar, Anthony or Adam Heilman, Johann Andreas Miller, Heinrich Haas, and Georg Kebner (fig. 1.5). On October 6, 1745, the church was consecrated and named Augustus, after the founder of the Halle Institutions, August Hermann Francke.[9]

The interior of the church, which could seat about 450 people, included a wineglass pulpit (fig. 1.6) and large balcony, which was supported by massive wooden columns. On the exterior, two wrought-iron weather vanes with the date "1743" adorned the roof (fig. 1.7) and were possibly made by Friedrich Marstellar, a blacksmith and one of the early deacons, whose name appeared on the date stone of the church. A third weather vane, dated "1750," was made for the schoolhouse erected by the congregation in that year to replace the original (fig. 1.8).[10] The church also acquired a pewter communion service with a baptismal bowl and flagon bearing the initials "A.D. H.M.," probably for Adam Heilman, who later became a warden of Zion's Church in Pikestown (built in 1751 and located in what is now East Pikeland Township, Chester County). Two chalices and a

Chapter One: Pastors

FIGURE 1.6
Pulpit of Augustus Lutheran Church. Long claimed to have been made of red walnut and imported from England, recent analysis has determined that the pulpit was constructed locally of American black walnut (*Juglans nigra*).

FIGURE 1.7
Weather vanes from Augustus Lutheran Church, 1743. Iron. Augustus Lutheran Church, Trappe, Pa.

FIGURE 1.8
Weather vane from schoolhouse of Augustus Lutheran Church, 1750. Iron. Augustus Lutheran Church, Trappe, Pa.

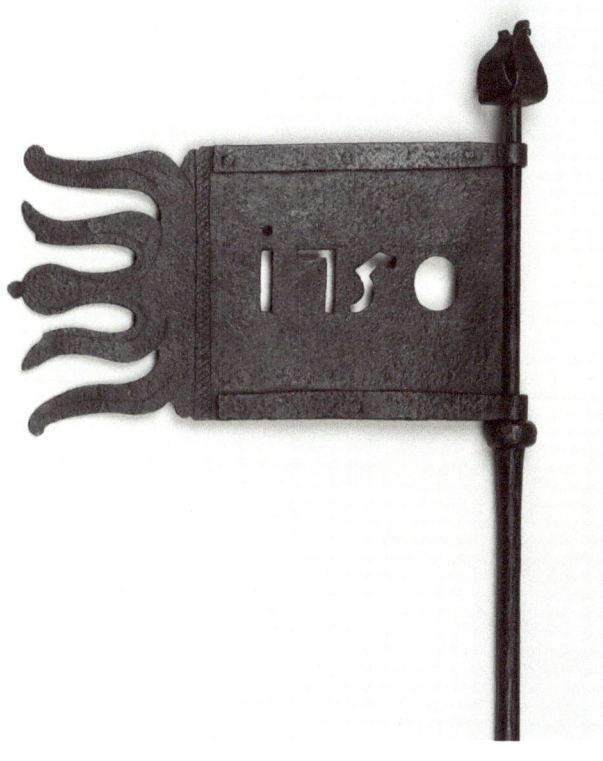

FIGURE 1.9
Communion service of Augustus Lutheran Church. Large flagon: attributed to Johann Philip Alberti (d. 1780), Philadelphia, c. 1760. Small flagon, probably Cologne, Germany, c. 1750. Chalices, probably Germany, c. 1750. Baptismal basin, probably England, c. 1750. Pewter. Augustus Lutheran Church, Trappe, Pa.

FIGURE 1.10
Communion flagon of New Hanover Lutheran Church, made by Gabriel Syren, Frankfurt-am-Main, Germany, c. 1750. Pewter. Inscribed "ANA MARGEREDA KERAUSSEN / DEN 6 APRIL 1750." New Hanover Lutheran Church, Gilbertsville, Pa.

second flagon, the latter made by Johann Philip Alberti of Philadelphia, were also acquired (fig. 1.9). In 1750, a pewter flagon was donated to the New Hanover congregation by Anna Margaretha Kerauss (fig. 1.10).[11] An organ was installed at Augustus in 1751, probably made by Johann Gottlob Clemm of Philadelphia. The organ, together with the construction of the organ loft, cost £123.15.4. The New Hanover Lutheran Church, by contrast, did not acquire an organ until 1802.[12]

Although Muhlenberg had been promised a regular salary as part of his call, he soon found that it was easier for most parishioners to pay him in kind. "I have no lack of things to eat and drink, God be praised," he wrote in 1743, "for one man brings me a sausage, another a piece of meat, a third a chicken, a fourth a loaf of bread, a fifth some pigeons, a sixth rabbits, a seventh eggs, an eighth some tea and sugar, a ninth some honey, a tenth some apples, an eleventh partridges, and so forth." Muhlenberg contented himself with this arrangement, noting "because we have heavy building programs in all three congregations . . . [I] want to spare the congregations so that it will not be too hard at the beginning." Three years later, he noted, "The dear people are glad to give corn, wheat, chickens, and the like, but money is rare." With his material needs thus provided, his major concern was that "I cannot preside over these three congregations indefinitely, for the work is too much and, besides, they are too widely separated. . . . Our primary need here is another pastor."[13] In January of 1745, Lutheran minister Peter Brunnholtz arrived from Halle, along with two catechists, Nicholas Kurtz and Johann Helfrich Schaum (both of whom were later ordained). In 1746, John Christopher Hartwick arrived from Hamburg. Additional ministers were sent from Halle in subsequent years, including John Frederick Handschuh (1748), John Diedrich Matthias Heinzelman (1751), Johann Ludwig Voigt (1764), Christopher Emanuel Schultze (1765), Justus Heinrich Christian Helmuth, Johann Friedrich Schmidt (1769), and John Christopher Kuntze (1770). Nonetheless, with more than 125 Lutheran congregations formed in Pennsylvania by 1776, serving them proved to be a continual challenge.[14]

Muhlenberg's congregation in Philadelphia had been worshipping in a rented building that he described as a "leaky slaughterhouse." Four months after his arrival, the congregation acquired a lot on Fifth Street at Appletree Alley and laid the cornerstone of a new church on April 5, 1743. The first public worship service was held there on October 20 although the building was far from complete. The church, known as St. Michael's, was not consecrated until August 14, 1748 (fig. 1.11). Built of brick and much larger than the Trappe church, it cost a total of £1,607.[15] Unfortunately, the steeple soon had to be removed. Swedish naturalist Peter Kalm described it as "having been put up by an ignorant builder before the walls of the church had become quite dry, the latter were forced out by its weight and the steeple had to be pulled down again in the autumn of the year 1750."[16] On May 12, 1751, St. Michael's dedicated an organ made by Johann Adam Schmahl of Heilbronn, Germany, a momentous event that included a dedication program printed by Benjamin Franklin and Johann Boehm.[17] Although St. Michael's could

FIGURE 1.11
Old Lutheran Church, in Fifth Street, Philadelphia, drawn and engraved by William Russell Birch (1755–1834) and Thomas Birch (1779–1851), 1800. From *Birch's Views of Philadelphia* (Philadelphia: W. Birch, 1800). Rare Book Department, Free Library of Philadelphia

FIGURE 1.12
Communion flagon of St. Michael's Lutheran Church, probably southern Germany, c. 1768. Pewter. Historical Society of Trappe, Collegeville, Perkiomen Valley, Inc.

FIGURE 1.13
Detail of inscription on the flagon illustrated in fig. 1.12.

seat about eight hundred people, it was soon overcrowded. A schoolhouse was built in 1761 to help provide additional space, and in October 1765 the pews of the front section were altered to accommodate more worshippers.[18] A pewter flagon and small domed-lid chest, inlaid with flowers and the Agnus Dei or Lamb of God, were among the early furnishings of the church (figs. 1.12–1.15).

The chest, which is made of American black walnut with maple and mahogany inlay, was probably made by a German émigré craftsman.[19]

Serving three separate congregations was no easy feat for Muhlenberg. Trappe and New Hanover were ten miles apart, with members of the congregations spread far and wide, and Philadelphia was some thirty miles southeast of Trappe. In addition to his regular Sunday services, baptisms, funerals, marriages, and visits to the sick, Muhlenberg also visited Lutheran congregations that were further afield, including Upper Milford and Saccum, Tulpehocken, Lancaster, York, and Raritan (New Jersey). In November 1748, he wrote to Halle about the situation. "I am worn out from much riding," he complained. "I am incapacitated for study; I cannot even manage my own household because I must be away most of the time." He implored the Fathers "to seek out a successor for me who will be able to relieve me and be a better support to my worthy brethren in the ministry." Not only was traveling exhausting, it could also be treacherous. On one particularly perilous crossing of the Perkiomen Creek, Muhlenberg's horse fell through the ice and nearly drowned.[20]

As the demands of his ministry grew, Muhlenberg found it increasingly difficult to remain single. "When there is only one hook in the house, everything is hung on it until it bends under the strain." A wife could help share the burden of his labor along with his joys. "Especially when my clerical brethren visited me," he wrote, "was such an attendance all the more necessary." He was also

beset with suggestions of eligible women from his parishioners, complaining, "I was often vexed at the great number of people who were concerned about securing my welfare through marriage." As the idea of marriage became an agreeable solution to his struggles, Muhlenberg sought a partner befitting his position. "Now, if I had gone ahead in the manner of the world and chosen wealth, I would very soon have become involved," he wrote in a letter to Halle. "As to the principle of selection," he added, "I considered nothing but sincere piety, such as might be convenable both for myself and my work. The Lord also regarded my prayers and granted me a young woman who is pure of heart, pious, simple-hearted, meek, and industrious."²¹ On April 15, 1745, he married Anna Maria or "Mary" Weiser (1727–1802), who was sixteen years younger. Mary's father, Conrad

FIGURE 1.14
Small chest, made for St. Michael's Lutheran Church, probably Philadelphia, c. 1750. American black walnut over hard pine with maple and mahogany; brass. Krauth Memorial Library, Lutheran Theological Seminary at Philadelphia

FIGURE 1.15
Detail of the lid of the chest illustrated in fig. 1.14. The slots are later additions, probably made to convert the chest for use as an alms or ballot box.

FIGURE 1.16
Portrait of Nicolaus Ludwig von Zinzendorf, Conrad Weiser, and five Iroquois Indians on August 2, 1742, by Anna Arndt, 1899, after Johann Valentin Haidt, c. 1742. Oil on canvas. Only known depiction of Conrad Weiser made during his lifetime; he is the man in the center with dark beard. The original painting by Haidt, owned by the Moravian Archives in London, was destroyed during World War II. Moravian Archives, Herrnhut GS 389

Weiser (1696–1760), was a leading figure in the Pennsylvania German community and an important ally for Muhlenberg. He was the primary liaison between the colonial Pennsylvania government and the Native Americans (fig. 1.16). In 1743, Weiser was appointed "province interpreter" and the following year helped to negotiate the Lancaster Treaty. Weiser was also a justice of the peace in Berks County and one of the founders of the town of Reading, which became the county seat in 1752.[22]

Henry Muhlenberg's marriage to Mary Weiser was a strategically important move in his efforts to build the Lutheran Church. Soon after the wedding, Henry visited his in-laws "for the purpose also of preparing my wife's brothers and sisters for confirmation and Communion." He noted that the Moravians were upset by the marriage, as they had hoped Mary would marry into their faith and thus bring her father into alliance with them, writing that "the whole affair was the occasion of much talk and gossiping,

 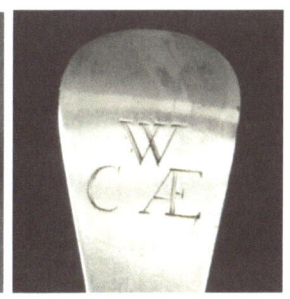

pro and con, throughout the country." Although Weiser was reared as a Lutheran, Henry said "matters were in such confusion in this country" that Weiser had "tried all sorts of [religious] persuasions," including the Society of Ephrata (later known as the Ephrata Cloister) and the Moravian Church.²³

Much is known about Weiser's life, but few artifacts survive that can be associated with him or his family though the probate inventory taken after his death reveals a well-furnished household. Included are a sizable library, silver watch, chamber organ, two corner cupboards, nine tables, and eighteen chairs. The small stone building on the outskirts of Womelsdorf, Berks County, on land once owned by Weiser, is now thought to be an early nineteenth-century structure. Weiser lived in Reading at the time of his death in 1760. His wife was Anna Eve Feg (c. 1705–81). Their initials are engraved on the back of a silver spoon made by Philadelphia silversmith Philip Syng Jr. (figs. 1.17 and 1.18) that was probably included in the "Fourteen large Silver Spoons" listed in the inventory and valued at £1 each. Anna Eve Weiser also owned a small European-made chest with elaborate parquetry veneer work that passed to her daughter Mary and descended in the Muhlenberg family (figs. 1.19 and 1.20). Though few, these objects speak to the prosperity of the Weiser family relative to that of most Pennsylvania Germans.²⁴

After their marriage, Henry and Mary settled in Trappe, where they built a two-story stone house (fig. 1.21). This substantial dwelling, which cost more than £200 to construct (provided by Conrad Weiser), was notably different from the small, one-story log houses occupied by most families in the area. As Henry had noted shortly after his arrival in 1742, "The people here in the country have

FIGURE 1.17
Spoon, owned by Conrad and Anna Eva Weiser, by Philip Syng Jr. (1703–89), Philadelphia, c. 1750. Silver. Two additional spoons from this set are owned by the Historical Society of Berks County Museum & Library, Reading, Pa., and the Pennsylvania Historical and Museum Commission. Lutheran Archives Center, Lutheran Theological Seminary at Philadelphia

FIGURE 1.18
Detail of engraving on back of spoon in fig. 1.17.

FIGURE 1.19
Small chest, owned by Anna Eve Weiser, probably continental Europe, c. 1725–50. Mixed-wood; brass. Descended from Anna Eve Weiser to her daughter Anna Maria (Weiser) Muhlenberg, then to her daughter Mary (Muhlenberg) Swaine, then to her sister Maria Salome (Muhlenberg) Richards, then to her daughter Mary Catharine (Richards) Myers, then to her brother John William Richards, then to his son Henry Melchior Muhlenberg Richards. Krauth Memorial Library, Lutheran Theological Seminary at Philadelphia

FIGURE 1.20
Detail of chest in fig. 1.19. Three small drawers are hidden by a removable panel (now missing) on the back.

FIGURE 1.21
House of Henry and Mary Muhlenberg, built 1745, Trappe, Montgomery County. Detail from a sketch made in 1851. Reproduced from Rev. Ernest T. Kretschmann, ed., *The Old Trappe Church: A Memorial of the Sesqui-Centennial Services of Augustus Evangelical Lutheran Church, Montgomery County, Pennsylvania* (Philadelphia: the church, 1893).

FIGURE 1.22
House of Henry and Mary Muhlenberg, built 1745, photo by S. R. Fisher, Norristown, Montgomery County, c. 1875. Courtesy of Pennypacker Mills, Montgomery County Department of Parks and Heritage Services, Schwenksville, Pa.

only one room in their houses, which is occupied by the whole family."25 Although the Muhlenbergs' house was later altered with the construction of a hip roof (fig. 1.22), the original plan contained a kitchen, stove room, and entry hall with stairs on the first floor. Germanic elements of its construction included the steep pitch and framing method of the original roof, use of stoves for heating, and paled insulation in the cellar joists. The house was built on an eighty-one-acre tract of land adjacent to the church property that Muhlenberg had purchased in 1744 from Johann Nicolaus Cressman. The Trappe congregation hoped to buy the house when they were in a better financial position and make it the permanent parsonage, but this never transpired, and Muhlenberg was burdened with debts for the land and household expenses. Notwithstanding the financial difficulties, he described the home lovingly and with no small sense of pride: "I now have a fairly good residence where I can raise the necessary grain for my bread, keep a horse and several head of cattle, and keep house with less trouble and work. . . . we rejoice that our home should be in Providence until we reach the true Fatherland and peace at last." In 1769, a description of the property noted seven acres of orchards, two kitchen gardens, a "never failing spring" on which a "wooden wash house" was erected, a "large stone barn and stable," and "having erected thereon a good two story stone messuage, with a convenient cellar under the same, and a well of good water in the cellar. Also a stone building annexed to the messuage, with a fire place therein."26

The sheer size and stone construction of the house projected the requisite message of authority and status needed for Muhlenberg to earn the trust of his parishioners and convince them to follow his lead. The parsonage became a community focal point to which the congregation looked for a model of piety and proper family life. Together with the church, it also served as a center of religious activities. In August 1748, Muhlenberg helped establish the Lutheran Ministerium of Pennsylvania, which had the authority to ordain ministers, make church constitutions, and try offenders against church discipline. At the first meeting, the group adopted a standard liturgy that included the order and content of Sunday morning worship services (to include several hymns, followed by a sermon of no more than one hour, Lord's Prayer, and hymn with offering) and occasional services

FIGURE 1.23
Carl Heinrich von Bogatzky, *Güldenes Schatz=Kästlein der Kinder Gottes* (Halle, 1761). Owned by Henry Melchior Muhlenberg, then descended in the family of his daughter Eve Elisabeth (Muhlenberg) Schultze to her great-granddaughter Margaretta Catharine Ermentrout (1836–94), who presented it in 1893 to her cousin John William Richards (1867–1944). Krauth Memorial Library, Lutheran Theological Seminary at Philadelphia

such as Holy Communion, baptisms, marriages, and funerals.[27] In June 1750, the ministerium held its annual meeting in Trappe. Seven pastors and sixty-three congregational delegates assembled at the Muhlenberg home, then "went in procession" to the church. Large crowds had been anticipated, so the windows were removed and "a shelter . . . with green branches" was erected around the church as the building "would scarcely hold half of the people who were present." Following the service, the Muhlenbergs "entertained the preachers and other good friends, as many as the house would hold." At the conclusion of the meeting on the second day, Henry wrote that "nearly eighty persons were given a meal at my place." At another ministerium meeting in 1760, the preachers and delegates assembled once more at the parsonage, where they received "nourishment for soul and body from Bogatsky's *Schatzkästlein* and from my patriarchal household." The *Schatzkästlein* (little treasure chest) was a small box of printed cards that contained daily spiritual verses (fig. 1.23). In the evening, the attendees met again at the house and were occupied with the "singing and playing of spiritual hymns" and edifying conversation until three o'clock in the morning.[28]

In addition to serving as a center of religious activity, the house also sheltered a growing family. Eight children were born to Henry and Mary in Trappe, beginning with the birth of Peter on October 1, 1746. When he began to teethe the following year, Henry wrote to his mother-in-law, asking her "to send a few wolves' teeth," which was a folklore remedy. Feeling the pinch of his unsteady income, Henry worried "now that I have a wife and son, and hence a household, and can hardly live on the income from the country congregations, it makes it very hard for me." In December 1750 he wrote, "My family was increasing to such an extent that, with children, servants, and maids, I had to keep about nine persons in daily food and clothing . . . not counting strangers and guests." He fretted that it was "impossible for my wife to manage the large household alone," resulting in "all sorts of disorders." The house was also a frequent stop for travelers, being described as "a sort of guest-house for the scattered." Henry's ministry frequently called him away from home, to the distress of his wife and family. On January 1, 1750, Mary gave birth to their third child, Frederick, during one of these absences. Henry's journal entry upon his return records that "in her anguish my wife wept over the fact that her husband was so seldom at home and that he was away just at this time. She felt that the wife of a workman or farmer was better off than she," he continued, "for they could at least be home most of the time. She resigned herself, however, to the fact that in this calling it cannot be otherwise." Fortunately for Mary, her father happened to stop by the house during her travail so she "had some visible support at any rate."29

In December 1750, Muhlenberg received a call to New York, which he accepted for a trial period of six months. Because the Pennsylvania congregations were fearful that he would not return, he left his family behind as security. Almost immediately upon his arrival in New York, Henry purchased new clothes, as he explained, "When I am at home in my country congregations I have to get along, just like the other peasants, with clothing which my wife spins and sews for me, as necessity teaches us to do. I would not dare wear such apparel here, however, unless I wanted the children on the streets to laugh at me behind my back." He soon learned that Mary was pregnant with their fourth child, and she insisted that he return home after three months. "Alas," he wrote, "he that is unmarried can better care for the things that belong to the Lord." Within several months of his return to Pennsylvania in August 1751 for the birth of Margaretta Henrietta, Henry went back to New York. He soon received "sharp letters from Pennsylvania—from my older colleagues and from my wife—which indicated that I should return to my congregations in Hanover and Providence and forsake New York." "In obedience to the command of my dear colleagues and the clamorous cries of my family," he returned to Pennsylvania.30

In 1761 Henry's ministerial duties called the family to Philadelphia, where the congregation had grown weary of their pastor living thirty-some miles away in the country. "I said to my wife on our arrival," Henry wrote, "that we would have to be prepared for suffering and distress." Two years later, they sold the Trappe property to Friedrich Martins, a "practitioner in physic," for

FIGURE 1.24
Pair of side chairs, owned by Henry and Mary Muhlenberg, attributed to Leonard Kessler (1737–1804), Philadelphia, 1763. Mahogany. Private collection; photo courtesy of Pook & Pook

£875. Henry and Mary acquired new furnishings for their Philadelphia household, including a set of mahogany chairs (fig. 1.24), for which they paid £10.2.6 in January 1763 to joiner Leonard Kessler, a member of St. Michael's church. The Trappe congregation began to complain about Henry's move to the city, prompting him to lecture them that they had applied to Germany for a preacher, promising a £40 annual salary, and that he had answered the call. He reminded them that as they had no parsonage, he had "built a house on it with his father-in-law's assistance, kept schoolmasters in his house, and supported them even after the congregation had built its own schoolhouse, etc. Now," he continued, "had the congregation also contributed its share of the £40 sterling annually, or had anyone even asked about it?" He concluded "that they should be satisfied with the catechist, like the congregation in New Hanover, until further insight and assistance should appear."[31]

In 1764 a "grievous cross was laid upon the family" when their seventh child, Johann Enoch Samuel, died in his sixth year. Samuel had been ill for more than a month when Henry observed that he "suffered a sudden attack of brain fever and violent convulsions and was so pitifully tormented that I thought he would give up the ghost." Fearful that God might be punishing him through the boy's illness, Henry "went into my chamber and committed my child into the hands of the most faithful Saviour, humbly acknowledging that I was aware of His intention, that I would kiss His fatherly rod of discipline, and that I would make the best possible use of it." The boy recovered briefly but took a sudden turn for the worse the following evening. Henry and Mary "sang several stanzas of the powerful Halle hymns for him" and told him "in accord with his little understanding, [about] the loving Saviour and heaven and blessedness." "Near ten o'clock, when I had him on my lap for the last time and was about to put him back in bed, he lovingly kissed me good-by, and after both of his parents had sung the hymn . . . he fell quietly asleep in his Redeemer." Henry was devastated by the loss. He "felt unfit for any kind of work" and prayed, "And now that it has pleased the all-gracious Saviour to order him out upon his last journey, I hope I shall soon follow." He felt a particular affinity for this child, "my baby son [who] was my traveling companion from the beginning of his life to the end of his pilgrimage." For his next sermon, Muhlenberg chose Matthew 18:6 as the text and preached on "the little ones . . . who believe in Jesus" at length.[32]

In April 1765, Muhlenberg received the distressing news that the New Hanover church had developed structural problems. During the service on Easter Sunday, the building "gave a loud crack and began to sink almost two feet on one side where the longest gallery is located." Those present "leaped out of the windows in terror, and the others rushed out of the doors . . . . This report," Henry wrote, "prophesies new burdens and troubles for me, since a new church must be built of stone in a time of the greatest lack of money and general scarcity."[33] A building committee was named soon after the incident, but it was not until June 25, 1767, that the cornerstone of the new church was laid and November 6, 1768, that it was dedicated (fig. 1.25). At the same time the New Hanover church was under construction, the

FIGURE 1.25
New Hanover Lutheran Church, built 1767, photo c. 1905, Gilbertsville, Montgomery County. Near the cornice is a stone inscribed by the master stonemason (*Mauer*): "M M / Michael Stofflet / 1767." Founded in 1717–18 by Anthony Henkel or possibly earlier by Daniel Falckner, New Hanover is the oldest German Lutheran congregation in Pennsylvania. New Hanover Lutheran Church, Gilbertsville, Pa.

FIGURE 1.26
New Lutheran Church, in Fourth Street Philadelphia, drawn and engraved by William Russell Birch (1755–1834) and Thomas Birch (1779–1851), 1799. From *Birch's Views of Philadelphia* (Philadelphia: W. Birch, 1800). During the 1790s when Philadelphia was the national capital, delegations of Indians visited to settle affairs with the federal government and were given tours of the city. This engraving, with Zion Lutheran Church in the background, is said to depict Frederick Muhlenberg conducting one such tour. Rare Book Department, Free Library of Philadelphia

Philadelphia congregation also embarked on a building campaign to help alleviate overcrowding at St. Michael's. A larger church, Zion Lutheran, was constructed between 1766 and 1769 on Fourth Street near the intersection with Arch Street (fig. 1.26). Designed by architect Robert Smith, Zion was an elegant brick structure adorned with Venetian windows, brick pilasters, and classical urns along the roof; it cost more than £9,500. With seating capacity for 2,500, it was one of the largest churches in the colonies and one of the largest public buildings in Philadelphia. During the American Revolution, a service of thanksgiving was held there after the surrender of Cornwallis in 1781, attended by members of Congress, the Pennsylvania Assembly, and Council. In 1786 the congregation contracted with Moravian organ builder David Tannenberg to construct what was the "largest and finest organ built in America" during the 1700s, for a cost of £1,500, excluding the case (which by one account measured 24 ft. wide x 27 ft. high). Large crowds of people attended the dedication of the organ on October 10–11, 1790. Tragically, a fire on December 26, 1794, caused part of the church roof to collapse (fig. 1.27) and gutted the interior, including the organ (although many of the organ pipes as well as the church library were saved). Tannenberg's offer to rebuild the organ for £3,000 was turned down, and it was not until 1811 that a new organ was completed. The church, however, was rebuilt and on December 26, 1799, became the site of George Washington's state memorial service as Philadelphia was then the national capital. By congressional decree, members of the military and clergy walked in front of a riderless horse and empty bier, followed by members of Congress in a procession from the State House (Independence Hall) to Zion Church. Bishop

William White, rector of Christ Church, led the service and "Light-Horse Harry" Lee of Virginia delivered the famous eulogy referring to Washington as "first in war, first in peace and first in the hearts of his countrymen." Sadly, Zion was torn down in 1869, one hundred years after its construction. St. Michael's suffered the same fate in 1872.[34]

The pressures of his extensive ministry weighed on Muhlenberg, who often struggled with feelings of inadequacy and depression. "Oh, how afraid I often become when I think of the heavy responsibility of the preacher's office and my own great unfitness for it," he wrote in 1750. Henry described his role as "not only shepherd and teacher, but often advocate, judge, physician, servant, and slave." When the demands on his person caused him to become ill, it was a matter of great concern, particularly when it affected his ability to preach. On one trip he described his "great embarrassment" over the loss of his voice: "When a preacher cannot speak, he is the poorest creature." The situation continued for several days and "was a bitter annoyance to me because the people are unrelenting and they are accustomed to judge a strange preacher by his physical health and strength." Muhlenberg also disliked being called upon to preach without time for preparation. On one occasion, he declined to conduct a funeral, noting "I cannot shake a funeral sermon out of my sleeve before such mixed, critical crowds." His stress was further compounded when asked to preach in English. In 1762, after being in America

FIGURE 1.27
Prospect Of the new Lutheran Church in Philad^a which was on the 26th of Dec. 1794 in the evening from the hour of eight till twelve Consumed by Fire, engraved by Frederick Reiche, 1795. Historical Society of Pennsylvania

for twenty years, he accepted one such request but "felt very uneasy because I have had only a little practice in the English language up to this time, and also because I have noted a marked loss of memory resulting from age and the many cares which weigh upon my mind."[35]

As Muhlenberg grew older, the demands of his ministry and extensive travels began to exert their toll. In April 1765, he was advised by a doctor to get more rest, but he felt it was impossible, "for I am in the same fix as a bird that the children have caught. They squeeze and roll it around until it is dead and then expect it to sing when it no longer has any breath." In September of that year he wrote, "Pennsylvania will miss me sorely when I die, for I am almost like a privy to which all those with loose bowels come running from all directions to relieve themselves." In 1766, he reluctantly agreed to travel to Lancaster to attend a church dedication, where he noted that the sermon was "imposed upon" him. Three years later, at the annual meeting of the ministerium over which Muhlenberg presided, the group reviewed a request from Tulpehocken to have Muhlenberg as their pastor. "This struck the meeting as ridiculous," he noted, "but it did not strike the president so, for there were entirely adequate grounds and reasons which might oblige and compel him to respond to this call."[36]

In addition to the near-constant travel, when Muhlenberg was at home, the household had "a constant siege of visitors." On one day in February 1763, he had "at least fourteen visits, one after another, from people of the congregations, this one complaining about something, that one inquiring, another quarreling, another delivering something or other, and so on." When heavy rain kept visitors away on another occasion, he wrote, "I was able, for once, to spend the entire day at home, alone, and devote my time to meditation and writing," but "in the evening I had visitors again." Pastors were also expected to make house calls, and Muhlenberg was frequently asked to perform weddings, funerals, and emergency baptisms, as well as attend to the sick or dying. Mary sometimes accompanied him, especially when they lived in Philadelphia. On a busy day in 1762 they left house at eight o'clock in the morning and together visited no fewer than eighteen individuals or families. At four o'clock they returned home, where a couple was waiting to be married. At seven they attended church with their children and sang hymns. From there Muhlenberg went to baptize a sick child and did not return until after ten o'clock.

FIGURE 1.28
Medicine bottles from Halle, c. 1750. Glass; enamel. Francke Foundations

Another time-consuming aspect of his duties was the voluminous correspondence he maintained with his fellow American pastors and European benefactors, which frequently kept him up late at night. Upon returning from a trip to New Jersey, he noted grimly that "a stack of letters from various parts of the country awaited my replies" and compared his "wretched correspondence" to a jail where prisoners are forced to turn a water wheel or drown. Because of the considerable time it took, "the good-hearted members of my family," Henry wrote, "often quarrel with me in love and say that I ruin my eyes and waste all my time scribbling." On his return from a preaching trip, Muhlenberg discovered that gossip had begun circulating that he intended to move away. After the church service, he admonished his congregation and told them that if he were planning to move, he would announce it publicly. "In the meantime," he stated, "I beg of you to let me alone and not disturb me in my difficult office."[37]

In addition to serving their parishioners' spiritual needs, ministers were often consulted about physical ailments and medical issues. In 1748 Muhlenberg let blood for two men and commented, "Since doctors are few and far between, I necessarily had to take a hand myself, having learned a little something while I was inspector in the infirmary at the blessed institutions." He later wrote, "Books and medicines belong to our concern and calling, the one for the soul and the other for the body." On numerous occasions, his "sage Opinion" was sought on issues that ranged from paralysis (for which he advised rubbing the patients' limbs with rattlesnake fat) to stab wounds to a broken leg. His affiliation with Halle, in addition to having provided him with some medical training, enabled him to import pharmaceutical goods as well as Bibles and other printed materials (figs. 1.28 and 1.29). Mary Muhlenberg also engaged in this trade. In 1772, Henry wrote, "With regard to the enclosed catalogue for books and medications, I note that my wife intends to continue the sale of the Halle medications, and although she has not yet used up her entire supply, she would at all times like to have stock on hand." On several occasions he noted that his wife was "cooking electuary," a syrup that was mixed with medicinal powders. Mary's pharmaceutical orders were paid and accounted for separately, probably using income from her substantial inheritance, which in 1785 was estimated at more than £1,000. From time to time she also made household purchases that Henry noted were out of "her money."[38]

Following the Muhlenbergs' move to Philadelphia in 1761, Henry had become concerned that the "impudent and emancipated youth" of the city would corrupt his oldest son, Peter, and cause "a great scandal and offense in my positions, and to the ruin of his own soul, if he should fall into wild ways." He knew that congregations looked to

FIGURE 1.29

Das Neue Testament (Halle, 1746). Marginal notes within the Bible are in Henry Melchior Muhlenberg's handwriting while the title page bears the signature of his granddaughter, Mary Catharine Richards (1785–1866), who later married Isaac Myers. Private collection

a pastor's family as an example for rearing their own children: "Members of congregations who love their pastor are likely to take their pastor's children as an example and think that what is permitted them is also proper and worthy of imitation by their own." He wrote to Court Preacher Ziegenhagen on January 10, 1762, to inquire of any positions in London for Peter "to learn surgery, or even an honest trade" or if the Halle institution might take him as a student. The reply came back that Halle would take not only Peter (aged sixteen) but his brothers Frederick (thirteen) and Henry Jr. (nine) as well. On April 27, 1763, the boys sailed for Europe. Two days after their departure, an anxious Henry noted, "I was feeling very ill the whole day and occupied with thoughts of death." They arrived safely in London on June 15, where they met Ziegenhagen, then visited their father's family in Einbeck, and finally traveled to Halle, where they arrived around September 1. Their course of study included Latin, Greek, Hebrew, and French as well as theology, general and ecclesiastical

FIGURE 1.30
St. Luke Lutheran Church, built 1765–67, photo c. 1880, Schaefferstown, Lebanon County. Henry Muhlenberg preached at the dedication of St. Luke in 1767 and described it as "one of the best in this land, built of massive stones, large, well laid out, and adorned with a tower." Historic Schaefferstown, Inc.

history, biblical criticism, and logic. Henry also requested that the boys "be practiced in singing, choral[e]s, and thorough bass on the piano." Peter was unhappy at Halle and was soon apprenticed to a merchant-apothecary in Lübeck for six years. In exchange, he was to receive instruction in keeping a business, Latin, and arithmetic. The situation proved less than ideal, however, and on August 14, 1766, Peter ran away, having secured a berth with a military regiment that was about to sail for America. The Halle fathers were infuriated. Francke wrote to Henry, "I heartily pity your Reverence for I can well conceive the sorrow which afflicts your old age . . . [and] hope that the prayers and tears of his beloved parents may bring back this erring son." Peter arrived in Philadelphia on January 15, 1767, and was enrolled in a "private English school . . . where he is learning bookkeeping, and making some progress. He keeps himself quiet and retired, yet is popular among friends." Peter considered going into business as an apothecary and sought to order pharmaceuticals from Halle, but Francke wrote that "they would not place any medicines from the Institution with such a one as Peter." Fortunately, Swedish Lutheran minister, Charles Magnus von Wrangel interceded and trained Peter to be a catechist, hiring a tutor to teach him Latin and Greek. Wrangel encouraged Peter to try preaching, which he did for the first time at St. Michael's on Good Friday in 1768.[39]

For six years Frederick and Henry Jr. continued their studies at Halle, but evidence suggests they were unhappy. In August 1769, Henry asked for them to be sent home. Johann Georg Knapp, who was briefly director in Halle after Francke's death in 1769, wrote their father in May 1770, "No real earnestness has been observed in them up to this time . . . indeed, on the contrary . . . their minds appear to incline to frivolity. Your Reverence will easily see yourself," he continued, "that it was not possible for me to vote that either one of them was fitted for the pastoral office, as I could not find the beginning of a change of heart in them, if the want of sufficient knowledge was overlooked."[40] On the heels of this admonition, the boys arrived in Philadelphia on September 26, along with John Christopher Kuntze, who would later marry their sister Margaretta Henrietta. On October 7, the

FIGURE 1.31
Three winged angel heads from St. Luke Lutheran Church, Schaefferstown, Lebanon County, c. 1767. White pine; paint. The angels were removed when the church was remodeled in 1884. Collection of Katharine and Robert Booth

Muhlenberg brothers preached their first sermon at Zion Lutheran Church to an audience of several thousand. On October 25 they were examined and ordained to the ministry. Frederick, who began a journal on the same day, wrote in the first entry: "This day is and always will be to me the most important day of my life, because on it I was ordained as a co-laborer in the United Evangelical Lutheran Congregations here." He was sent to serve in the Tulpehocken region, some seventy miles from Philadelphia, where his congregations included Warwick, White Oak, and Heidelberg or Schaefferstown (figs. 1.30 and 1.31). Henry Jr. labored briefly in New Jersey before returning to Philadelphia to assist his father with some of the outlying congregations. Peter, who was not yet ordained, was invited on May 4, 1771, to a Lutheran church in Woodstock, Virginia. One of the conditions of the call was that he be ordained by a bishop of the Church of England, which was the state church of Virginia. He sailed to London on March 2, 1772, and on April 25 was ordained by the Bishop of London at King's Chapel (fig. 1.32). By August he had returned to Pennsylvania and had begun preparing to move to Woodstock, the seat of the newly

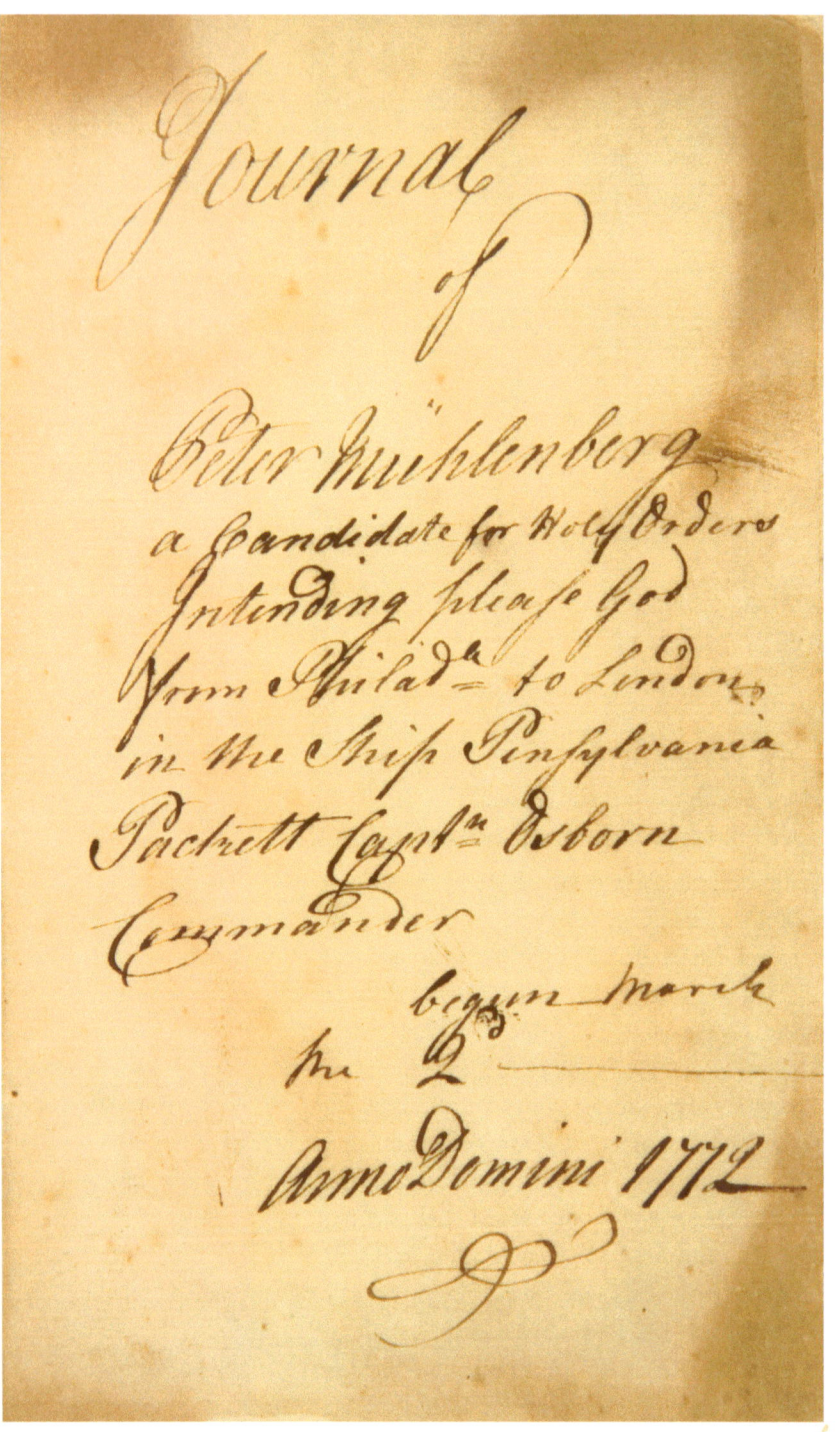

FIGURE 1.32
Journal kept by Peter Muhlenberg en route to England in 1772. Collection of a descendant

established Dunmore County and an area of heavy German settlement.⁴¹

Thus, the three Muhlenberg brothers joined their father in the Lutheran ministry. With Peter now living in the Shenandoah Valley of Virginia, Henry used his seniority in the church to keep his other sons closer to home. When a Maryland congregation petitioned to have Frederick become their pastor in 1772, Henry flatly refused and said that "my son Friedrich was already living eighty miles away from me and that, if he should be twice as far away, I could expect little or no assistance from him in my weary old age." He twice deflected efforts to call Henry Jr. away, writing that "I myself needed him and he was absolutely indispensable in giving me help and support." When a congregation in New Germantown, New Jersey, tried to persuade Henry to let his son accept a call there, again he declined and wrote, "As far as my son, Henry, is concerned, I need him for my own support in my weakness."⁴²

Try as Henry did to keep his children close to home, the second generation was fast growing up and starting out on their own. On November 6, 1770, Peter married Anna Barbara or Hannah Meyer (1751–1806) of Philadelphia, who moved with him to Woodstock two years later. Frederick married Catharine Schaeffer (1750–1835) on October 15, 1771. Her father, David, was a prominent sugar refiner in Philadelphia and longtime elder at St. Michael's Lutheran Church. The young couple settled in Schaefferstown, where Frederick preached until 1773, when he accepted a call to Christ Lutheran Church in New York City. Henry Jr. married Catherine Hall (1756–1841) on July 26, 1774. In 1780, he accepted a call to Trinity Lutheran Church in Lancaster (fig. 1.33), where he served as pastor for thirty-five years and lived in the parsonage, a stone house that still stands at 33 North Duke Street (fig. 1.34). From 1785–94, a steeple was added to the church with carved wooden statues of the four evangelists at the corners. Soon after its completion, traveler Theophile Cazenove noted: "The new German Lutheran church is very well built, of brick, and its steeple is the best built and the most elegant one in the United States. It is a pity," however, "that the immense statues of the 4 Evangelists are too small by half."⁴³

Of the Muhlenbergs' four daughters, the eldest two married Lutheran ministers. In 1766 Eve Elisabeth (1748–1808) married Christopher Emanuel Schultze (1740–1809), who arrived from Halle in 1765. Peter Muhlenberg presented them with a tilt-top mahogany tea table as a wedding present, possibly the "Mohockony Table" or "round Table" listed in Emanuel's inventory of 1809. After living for several years in Philadel-

Chapter One: Pastors

FIGURE 1.33
Trinity Lutheran Church, built 1761–66, by E. R. Hammond, Lancaster, 1845. The steeple addition was completed in 1794. Evangelical Lutheran Church of the Holy Trinity, Lancaster, Pa.

FIGURE 1.34
House of Henry Muhlenberg Jr., built c. 1750, Lancaster. LancasterHistory.org, Lancaster, Pa.

phia, the Schultzes moved to Tulpehocken in 1771 and settled into the parsonage at Christ Lutheran Church near Stouchsburg, Berks County (figs. 1.35 and 1.36). The second daughter, Margaretta Henrietta (1751–1831), married Lutheran minister John Christopher Kuntze (1744–1807) in 1771 (figs. 1.37 and 1.38), less than a year after he had accompanied Frederick and Henry Jr. on their voyage home from Germany. The Kuntzes initially lived in Philadelphia, where Rev. Kuntze taught German and Hebrew at what is now the University of Pennsylvania (fig. 1.39). They moved to

FIGURE 1.35
Signature album, owned by Eve Elisabeth Muhlenberg Schultze, 1771–1808. Contains entries from her parents and other family members dated just prior to her removal from Philadelphia to Tulpehocken on January 28, 1771. Muhlenberg College, Special Collections and Archives

FIGURE 1.36
Christ Lutheran Church, built 1786, photo c. 1910, near Stouchsburg, Berks County. Collection of Mr. and Mrs. Michael Emery

FIGURES 1.37 and 1.38
Portraits of Margaretta Henrietta Muhlenberg Kuntze and John Christopher Kuntze, c. 1790. Whereabouts unknown; reproduced from Henrietta Meier Oakley and John Christopher Schwab, *Muhlenberg Album* (New Haven, Conn.: the authors, 1910)

FIGURE 1.39
Bookplate of John Christopher Kuntze, from Johann Jacob Rambach, *Schrifftmäßige Erläuterung der Grundlegungden Theologie* (Frankfurt: Wolfgang Ludwig Spring, 1738). Krauth Memorial Library, Lutheran Theological Seminary at Philadelphia

FIGURES 1.40 and 1.41
Portraits of Maria Catharine Muhlenberg Swaine and Francis Swaine, probably Pennsylvania, c. 1790. Oil on canvas. Collection of a descendant

New York in 1784, where Kuntze became pastor of Christ Church and taught at Columbia University.[44]

The two younger Muhlenberg daughters parted with tradition by not marrying Lutheran ministers. Maria Catharine (1755–1812), known as Mary, married Francis Swaine (1754–1820), an Irish immigrant, on August 9, 1775 (figs. 1.40 and 1.41).[45] Henry gave his new son-in-law a copy of the *Book of Common Prayer* as a present soon after the wedding (figs. 1.42 and 1.43). In 1779, while living with her parents, Mary gave birth to their first child, George Washington Swaine. The Swaines had three more children, but all died during childhood. However, Mary worked as a nurse and midwife, aiding Frederick's wife, Catharine, in the delivery of their sixth child in December 1782. Following the end of the Revolution in 1783, Henry wrote to Francis Swaine's father in Ireland. He noted the reply with approval, "Being now convinced of the young man's Descent from Honest and Christian Parents . . . we can more prop[erly] join Heart and Hand."[46] After several rather unsuccessful stints in the military, including an appointment as clothier of the state of Pennsylvania in 1779, Francis became a storekeeper in Trappe. From 1787 to 1790 he was sheriff of Montgomery County. In 1800 he was made prothonotary of the court of common pleas and moved to Norristown, the county seat. Twelve years later he was elected the first burgess (mayor) of that town and in 1815 became the first president of the Bank of Montgomery County.[47] The youngest Muhlenberg daughter, Maria Salome, or Sally (1766–1827), was married in 1782 to Matthias Reichert or Richards (1758–1839), a young widower, prosperous saddler, and member of the New Hanover church (figs. 1.44 and 1.45). Henry Muhlenberg performed the ceremony, which was followed by a modest wedding feast that included a dinner of veal. Matthias served in the Revolutionary War and later became a congressman from 1807 to 1811.[48]

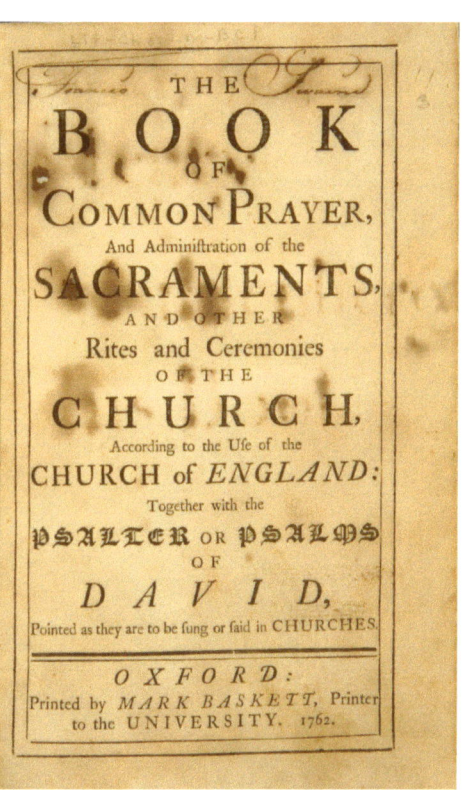

FIGURES 1.42 and 1.43
Inscriptions and title page of *The Book of Common Prayer* (London: Mark Baskett, 1762). Krauth Memorial Library, Lutheran Theological Seminary at Philadelphia

FIGURES 1.44 and 1.45
Portraits of Maria Salome Muhlenberg Richards and Matthias Richards, probably Pennsylvania, c. 1790. Whereabouts unknown; reproduced from Henrietta Meier Oakley and John Christopher Schwab, *Muhlenberg Album* (New Haven, Conn.: the authors, 1910).

FIGURE 2.1
Detail of portrait of Peter Muhlenberg in fig. 2.6. Collection of Brian and Barbara Hendelson

CHAPTER TWO
PATRIOTS

*I*n August 1774, Henry Muhlenberg traveled from Philadelphia to Ebenezer, Georgia, to settle a dispute in the congregation. Mary, who by this time had developed a debilitating illness that caused her to have seizures, accompanied him as did their daughter Mary. By the time of their return to Philadelphia in March 1775, talk of Revolution was rampant, and rumors were circulating that Muhlenberg had left town because he was a Tory sympathizer. In December Henry observed, "it seems that the flames of war will spread . . . during the coming year" and feared they would lay waste to Philadelphia. Little did he know that his son Peter (fig. 2.1) would soon become immersed in the conflict. He reflected that "if I still had my farm in Providence, one or another of my fleeing colleagues might, in addition to myself, find refuge there." Mary's illness had also become more severe since their return, and she wrote to their daughter Elisabeth, "So I am convinced that the city is much to blame for it, and sincerely wish that Papa would have moved to some place in the country, or to Reading with my mother. He also promised me," she continued, "when we were in Ebenezer that if my sickness were to get worse and if he could be released, he wanted to do it." While "troubled by such thoughts," Henry "happened by chance" upon an advertisement for a property in Providence or Trappe. "The property," he wrote, "consists of seven to eight acres adjacent to the street, most of it laid out in orchards and vegetable gardens." In addition, there was "a large two-story dwelling, built of massive stones . . . with four rooms on the lower and four on the upper floor. Nearby is a one-story stone house and workshop, together with two draw-wells and a large stone barn and stables." Taking this as a sign, he "resolved to buy the place" and on January 1, 1776, executed the bill of sale.[1]

Built by Jacob Schrack II about 1750, the house was well known to Henry, who estimated that it had cost Schrack more than £500 to construct (fig. 2.2). A blacksmith by trade, Schrack suffered from mental illness and in 1764 was hospitalized in Philadelphia.[2] After returning to Trappe, he unsuccessfully tried to rent and then sell the property, which was finally put up for sheriff's sale in 1769. The property passed through several hands and was in poor condition when the Muhlenbergs acquired it. David Schaeffer, Frederick's father-in-law, contributed £100 to the purchase so that Frederick "might in an emergency flee thither with his wife and children and might enjoy shelter." To this Henry added £200 from a legacy for pastors and £40 contributed by Mary, part of her inheritance from her father. In March 1776, Henry traveled to Trappe with a housekeeper, Widow Zimmerman, to take possession of the property. Finding the house uninhabitable, he left her with neighbors and hired workers to "clear out the large house and remove the heaviest dirt." He then paid a joiner for installing thirty-eight windowpanes and hired laborers for "whitewashing and cleaning the rooms, kitchen, and hallways, and also cleaning the cellar." Two hundred trees in the orchard were pruned. After contracting to have the fences mended, Henry left the property in the hands of Widow Zimmerman and returned to Philadelphia, where war seemed imminent. On July 2, his son Frederick arrived in Philadelphia, having fled there from New York. Two days later, Henry wrote on July 4 that "today the Continental Congress openly declared the united provinces of North America to be free and independent states . . . the end will show who played the right tune" (fig. 2.3). One week later, on July 11, Henry, his wife, and youngest daughter, Sally, left Philadelphia and moved to Trappe.[3]

Numerous repairs and improvements were made to the house in the following year, including the installation of stoves with pipes and a stone addition that combined the functions of washhouse, storeroom, bake house, and extra kitchen. In November, Henry "urged the carpenter and mason to redouble their efforts because I must take in several families from the city." The "small adjoining house" that was attached to the main house was occupied throughout the war by various family members or rented out to tradesmen. By

FIGURE 2.2
House of Henry and Mary Muhlenberg, 1776–87, then Peter Muhlenberg, 1787–1802, built c. 1750 for Jacob Schrack II, Trappe, Montgomery County. Historical Society of Trappe, Collegeville, Perkiomen Valley, Inc.

mid-December, Henry reported that "wagons filled with household goods, men, women, and children fleeing from Philadelphia went by all day." As the year 1776 drew to a close, he meditated upon his favorite hymn, *Ich armer Sünder komm zu dir mit demütigen Herzen* (I poor sinner come to you with a humble heart). Chief among his concerns were his own age, his wife's illness, and the many people dependent upon him for support. "Around me in our dwelling," he wrote,

> I have a daughter not yet of age, a nurse for my wife, and a maidservant; in the adjoining apartments, two sons' wives, four small grandchildren, a devout mother-in-law of one of my sons, and two maidservants; and in the adjoining cottage a female relative with four little children, a manservant and a maidservant, and off and on my two sons, Friedrich and Heinrich. . . . When they are all together, there are twenty-two souls under one roof.

On January 2, 1777, the arrival of another family brought the total to "thirty souls in our 'hospital.'" This level of crowding was not unusual during the war years. In 1780 Henry wrote that the "little household is crawling and teeming." His count of "stomachs and mouths" included "(a) we two old folks and one adolescent daughter, Salome; (b) the general, his wife, three menservants, two children, and one negress; (c) Mr. Sw[aine], his wife, and one child." He added, "The appendix contains twenty some chickens, three dogs, and two cats," as well as seven horses, three cows, and three calves. The crowded conditions, noise, smells, and general hubbub of the household can scarcely be imagined. In addition to all of the inhabitants, the rooms were packed with furnishings and household goods sent for safekeeping by the Muhlenberg children and their relatives. On other occasions, the family sent valuable goods to the Schultzes at Tulpehocken for safekeeping, including a trunk filled with Henry's books and papers, bed and window curtains, and various articles of clothing, including two silk gowns and one cotton gown belonging to Mary.[4]

As the conflict with England developed, Muhlenberg found that his loyalties were divided. As a native of the Electorate of Hanover and a British subject who had sworn an oath of allegiance to the Hanoverian King George of England, he felt a dual allegiance, but as a resident of Pennsylvania for more than thirty years he could also sympathize with the attitudes of the Revolutionaries. Many writers have delved into Muhlenberg's beliefs vis-à-vis the American Revolution. Early biographers tended to claim that Henry was a fervent patriot and strong supporter of his sons Peter and Frederick, both of whom ultimately left the ministry to aid the Revolutionary cause. Other historians wrote that Henry "pursued a thorny path of exceedingly difficult neutrality," feeling obligated as a minister to refrain from choosing sides.[5] Muhlenberg's own words and actions reveal that he intentionally did not voice his personal opinions too loudly, though as the senior pastor of the Lutheran Ministerium he would have had plenty of opportunity to do so.

FIGURE 2.3

Eine Erklärung durch die Repräsentanten der Vereinigten Staaten von America (Philadelphia: Melchior Steiner and Carl Cist, 1776). Deutsches Historisches Museum, Berlin

Muhlenberg did find it difficult to remain publicly neutral, writing in October 1784 after the war that "if as preacher one wished to be neutral, one got caught between two fires." He frequently claimed ignorance of political affairs, noting that "my call was limited to the welfare of souls and I could not engage in any political activity whatsoever." On another occasion, "I have had little or nothing to do with political affairs, and it is not my sphere even now, as my office is concerned with other things." After giving a word of admonition to a local battalion in August 1776, Henry observed that "ministers neither can nor should be judges or arbitrators in such a conflict" and should submit the matter to God, the "only and highest Judge of heaven and earth." In spite of these sentiments, he had preached a sermon of thanksgiving when the Stamp Act was repealed in August 1766. The previous year, however, he had refused to muffle the bells on the Lutheran schoolhouse "and toll them in mourning" to protest the Stamp Act (fig. 2.4), and advised his parishioners to "remain quiet" and avoid engagement. Despite the ambiguities of his opinion on the Revolution, Henry paid close attention to the events of the war, and his journal entries record detailed information such as casualty numbers, battlefield outcomes, and transcriptions of speeches both in favor of and against the conflict. At the beginning of the war, his journal entries include comments sympathetic to both sides. In September 1777, for example, he wrote that because of inclement weather "the poor men of both armies are in a bad way, for they must be out in the cold wind and rain, without tent or roof, and thinly clothed." Several months later, he noted thankfully that "since July, 1776 I have accordingly lived in seclusion . . . that I have not been obliged to become involved in politics and that I have been able to retain the liberty of praying for all men." Muhlenberg's self-imposed clerical neutrality, however, seems to have slowly receded by the end of the war. In 1778 he wrote admiringly that "according to the ancient Roman fashion," referring to the legendary farmer-general Cincinnatus, who after war returned to his fields, "In time of peace the American officer wears his own hair as it is grown, wears clothing in keeping with his occupation, and when the need arises to fight for his rights and liberties, he beats his plowshare and sickle into a spear and sword."[6] After reading a German translation of Thomas Paine's *Common Sense* (fig. 2.5), he sent a copy to his son-in-law Emanuel Schultze at Tulpehocken and commented in the accompanying letter of March 7, 1776: "The young people are right in fighting for their God-given native liberty."[7] When his son Peter wrote to him in November 1778 seeking advice regarding "a conflict of two important duties"—namely, that Peter's wife, Hannah, was pregnant and desired him to come home although his military duties called him elsewhere—Henry advised his son to "weigh the circumstances and arrange them in the proper order, giving the preference to the . . . common welfare over the private." He urged Peter to "remain at your post," or "hundreds and [thousands] of his fellowmen may be neglected, ruined, and lost" and "a crafty and powerful enemy cannot be restrained by midwives."[8]

Henry Muhlenberg's primary moral challenge with regard to the Revolution was that as a minister he believed God was the Supreme Ruler above all temporal authorities, citing from Romans 13: "Let every soul be subject unto the higher powers which have authority over you and protect you" and Daniel 2: "God, who rules over all things . . . removeth kings and setteth up kings according to His most holy will."[9] On this basis, Muhlenberg was prepared to accept whatever outcome might

FIGURE 2.4
Teapot, probably Staffordshire, England, 1766–70. Creamware. Objects such as this teapot, inscribed "No Stamp Act" and "American Liberty Restored," were used by American colonists to denounce the tax and celebrate its repeal in 1766. Private collection; photo courtesy of Winterthur Museum

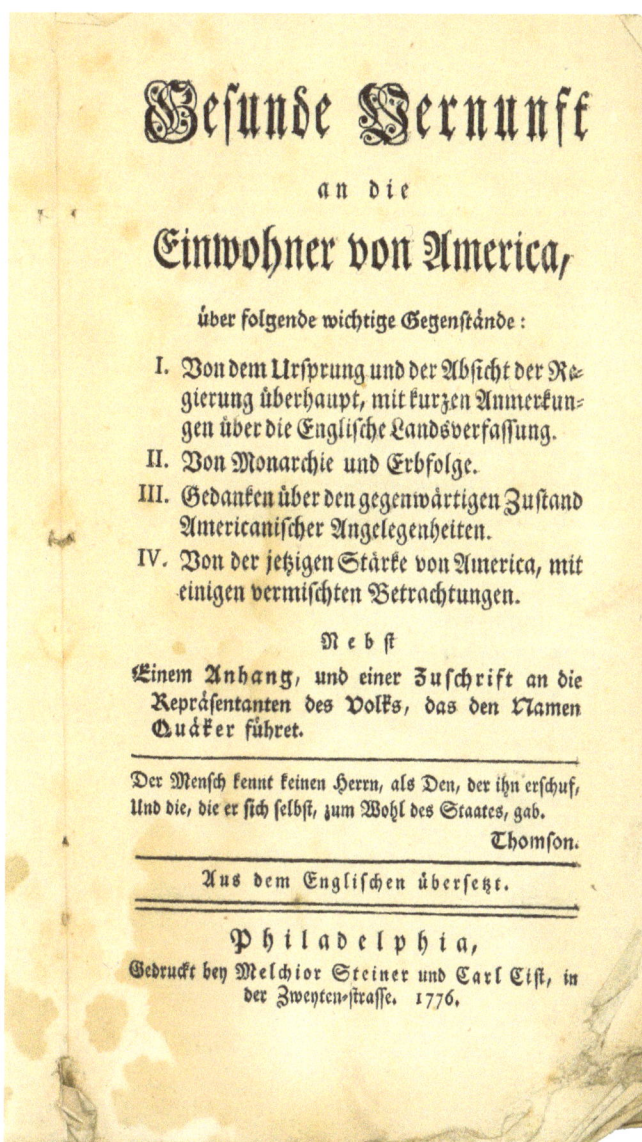

FIGURE 2.5
Thomas Paine, *Gesunde Vernunft an die Einwohner von America* (Philadelphia: Melchior Steiner and Carl Cist, 1776). American Philosophical Society

FIGURE 2.6
Portrait of Peter Muhlenberg, after John Trumbull (1756–1843), probably Pennsylvania, c. 1800–1825. Oil on canvas. Collection of Brian and Barbara Hendelson

transpire as God's will, and his journals are replete with commentary expressing a continued adherence to this viewpoint. In the early stages of the war, on January 4, 1777, he wrote, "America needs and deserves God's rod of correction and punishment. Yet it is to be regretted that England has so degenerated that the Lord God finds it a fit agent to serve as disciplinarian and executioner over its own daughter." Four years later, on learning of the American victory at Yorktown in 1781, he noted, "The sublime Saviour has accepted a prevailing intercession for the unfruitful fig tree in his vineyard, and has allowed that it should not yet be hewn down." With the war nearly over, Henry wrote in March 1783 that "one can, of course, reasonably conclude from this success that it was the will of the Supreme Ruler of heaven and earth that there should be independence." He worried, however, that "many do not understand the word independence, and do not want to understand it, because they think that now they are also independent of the Saviour of the world and His laws and are left to themselves."[10]

From his vantage point in Trappe, Henry had witnessed the events of the Revolution unfold. Miles away in Virginia his son Peter became drawn into the conflict (fig. 2.6). On June 16, 1774, Peter chaired a meeting of Woodstock inhabitants who drew up a series of resolutions protesting the so-called Intolerable Acts and formed a Committee of Correspondence, of which he was elected chair. In August, he was one of two representatives

FIGURE 2.7
Clerical robe, tradition of ownership by Peter Muhlenberg, Pennsylvania or Virginia, c. 1770–75. Silk and wool. Krauth Memorial Library, Lutheran Theological Seminary at Philadelphia

from Dunmore County sent to the Virginia Convention in Williamsburg. In January 1775, he was re-elected chairman of the Committee of Correspondence and Safety and in March attended the convention at which Patrick Henry delivered his famous "give me liberty, or give me death" speech. On January 12, 1776, Peter accepted a commission as a colonel of the Eighth Virginia Regiment and began raising troops among the Germans in the Shenandoah Valley. According to legend, he delivered a rousing farewell sermon in Woodstock, probably on January 21, based on Ecclesiastes 3:1-8, "to every thing there is a season, and a time to every purpose under the heaven." In the most colorful versions of this story, after exhorting his congregation that "there is a time for all things—a time to preach and a time to fight, and now is the time to fight!" Peter threw off his clerical robe to reveal his military uniform underneath and promptly began mustering volunteers. The story may have some truth to it. Dr. James Thacher, an army surgeon who attended a dinner party Peter hosted on November 3, 1778, later wrote that Peter had "exchanged his clerical profession for that of a soldier . . . [and] entered his pulpit with his sword and cockade, preached his farewell sermon, and the next day marched at the head of his regiment to join the army."[11] An eighteenth-century clerical robe, which was carefully preserved by the Henkel family of Virginia, through whom it descended, is said to be the robe worn on that fateful day (fig. 2.7). Whatever transpired during Peter's last sermon, the legend of the "fighting parson" has become a popular story, and images of Peter Muhlenberg in the act of disrobing have adorned everything from statues to stained-glass windows to a large water tower outside Woodstock to the cover of children's books (fig. 2.8). A flag from the Eighth Virginia Regiment, now faded from its original salmon-red color, has been passed down among Peter's descendants (fig. 2.9).[12]

Henry Muhlenberg makes no mention of this incident in his journals, but he was probably not overly surprised by the turn of events. In 1763, soon after Peter had sailed for Germany, Henry sent a letter to Ziegenhagen and Francke saying that "unfortunately my boy Peter enjoyed very little care and supervision from me, owing to the distractions of my pastoral duties." "His chief fault and evil bent," Henry continued, "was toward hunting and fishing." If Peter caused any trouble, Henry wrote, "I humbly beg you to put him in some place where there are disciplined soldiers . . . under the name of Peter Weiser . . . there he can obey the sound of the drum if he will not follow the Spirit of God." By early March 1776, Frederick had learned of Peter's enlistment, and he wrote a letter to his brother Henry Jr. in Philadelphia expressing concern over the situation. Henry Jr. forwarded the letter to Peter, who fired off an epistle to Frederick denouncing him as a Tory. Although

Peter's letter is lost, Frederick's response, which he transcribed in the back of his journal, concluded by saying,

> I think you are wrong for trying to be both soldier and preacher together. Be one or the other. No man can serve two masters. . . . I incline to think a preacher can with good conscience resign his office and step into another calling. You think a man can be both preacher and colonel at the same time. . . . You ought to . . . hold fast to that important office entrusted to you, and provided you are convinced of the legitimacy of our cause, there is plenty of opportunity to contribute your part to the good of liberty in your profession.

Frederick then proceeded to defend his own views, writing "I think I have always been as steadfast as you in our American cause . . . although I am not colonel and do not take the field." Not surprisingly, Henry was none too pleased with

FIGURE 2.8
Arthur H. Kuhlman, *Pulpit and Battlefield: A Story of Peter Muhlenberg and the American Revolution* (Columbus, Ohio: The Book Concern, [1923]). Private collection

FIGURE 2.9
Flag of the Eighth Virginia Regiment, later owned by Peter Muhlenberg, c. 1776–78. Silk. Collection of a descendant; photo courtesy of Winterthur Museum

Peter's decision to leave the ministry. On learning of Peter's promotion to the rank of brigadier general in 1777, he warned, "The higher you climb . . . the more dangerous the fall."[13]

Although Trappe was never the site of a battle, during the fall of 1777 it was the site of much military activity. At first Henry complained primarily of the noise, writing, "Here I thought I should have a solitary, quiet, private life, but I have still continued to live in commotion since all sorts of invasion and marchings through are occurring constantly." As the violence of the war escalated, however, he began to receive reports via the newspapers and letters from family members of "bloody and barbarous goings-on" that caused him far greater concern. During the Battle of the Brandywine on September 10–11, Henry wrote in his journal that they "heard heavy and long cannonading some thirty miles away on Brandywine Creek." On September 19, the Americans crossed the Schuylkill River at Parker's Ford and marched four miles to Trappe to connect with the Great Road that ran from Philadelphia to Reading, directly in front of the Muhlenbergs' house. All night long the road teemed with troops, horses, and cannon. "At midnight a regiment camped in the street in front of my house," Henry reported. "Some vegetables and chickens were taken, and a man with a flint came to my chamber, demanded bread, etc." The next day Mary and her daughters baked bread for the soldiers. By September 25, the British had taken Philadelphia. The same day, General Anthony Wayne, Lord Stirling, and several aides-de-camp called on the Muhlenbergs and dined in their house.[14]

For months after the fall of Philadelphia, rumors circulated that made Henry fearful of a British raid or attack by Hessian soldiers. "It is charged against me," he wrote, "that one of my sons is an officer in the opposing party. That is true, but he is no longer under my control and command; he was two hundred and fifty miles away from me and entered contrary to my will and warning." In December 1777, he wrote, "I am told on all sides that the English and Hessian officers have singled me out for revenge and that they will have me captured by their dragoons at the first opportunity. . . . Everyone advises me to get out of the way. But where should I go? I have a sick wife, am myself old and feeble." A subsequent report that the British army was within seven miles of Trappe "brought fresh terror" to the household. After the danger had passed, Henry wrote thankfully, "When one looks upon one's family, house, home, and life after danger has threatened and been turned away, it is like an undeserved gift." Although Henry frequently considered seeking refuge with family members who lived further in the country, the severity of Mary's illness and desire to remain in her own home induced them to stay. On February 25, 1778, Muhlenberg "received the dreadful news that the British light cavalry was near us and that we would be attacked tonight. I had nine weak women and four children under my roof," he continued, "so I fled secretly to Jesus Christ and stayed up until four o'clock in the morning. The Lord was our defense and shelter, and we met with no attack. They did not carry old M[uhlenberg] away with them." The worries continued the next evening, with the report that the "British cavalry is coming nearer and nearer . . . and were going to take me." Muhlenberg agonized over his helplessness but felt unable to do anything, writing, "I cannot flee, much less leave my sick wife behind, so I must await whatever God's holy providence . . . has ordained for me." Although Muhlenberg's concerns proved unnecessary as he was never taken prisoner, his fears were not unfounded. His counterpart in the German Reformed church, Michael Schlatter, was imprisoned for five months in Philadelphia by the British, who also destroyed Schlatter's house, furnishings, books, and papers.[15]

In October 1777, Muhlenberg wrote that "our house, kitchen, and barn are already filled with soldiers who are seeking shelter and want to get dry." The following month he was approached by Robert Dill, commissary in the American army, with a request to store supplies in the cellar, said to be "the largest and best cellar in this neighborhood." Muhlenberg "did not dare refuse," calling it his "duty to serve friends and foes as one can." In December, on hearing that the Continental army had moved across the Schuylkill River to Valley Forge for the winter, he wrote, "We are now living in constant expectation of an attack from Philadelphia as the American army has gone into winter quarters... and left the pass open." The army had also left its mark on Trappe. Soldiers returning from the battle of Ticonderoga were quartered in the house of Henry's neighbor, Johannes Ried. Crops were trampled, fences broken and burned for firewood, gardens and livestock pillaged. Ten acres of woodland that Henry had bought near the church were laid to waste, and he reported that at his former home in Trappe the soldiers had "wrought havoc on the place" by breaking furniture and smashing fences. The worst abuse was at Augustus Lutheran Church, which the Pennsylvania militia seized in September 1777. When Henry entered the church on September 27 to prepare for a funeral, he found the building "crowded with officers and privates with their guns.... one man was playing the organ while others sang to his accompaniment. Down below lay straw and manure, and several had placed the objects of their gluttony, etc. on the altar." When Henry's presence was noted, "they at once began to jeer and several officers called up to the organ-player, 'Play a Hessian march.'"[16] Despite his son Peter's role in the Continental army, Henry's German birth and disinclination to publicly declare his opinions about the war led some to suspect him of harboring sympathies for the German King George and his Hessian mercenaries.

By 1779, Frederick Muhlenberg began to consider leaving the ministry and going into business. On hearing rumors of this, his brother-in-law, Christopher Kuntze, wrote to Henry, saying "Can it be, dear Father, that Brother Friedrich intends to give up his ministry and become a merchant?... It is said that he cannot make ends meet. I still think, however, that this only means that he cannot get rich." He concluded, "I hope that you will not give your consent thereto.... I wish that regard for you may prevent it." A different opportunity arose, however, as Frederick's name was soon put forth as a candidate to fill a vacancy in the Continental Congress. On February 15, Henry wrote, "It is said that the Assembly now in session wishes to appoint three additional members to Congress, and some of them have proposed Fried[rich] M[uhlenberg] because he understands both English and German."[17] Frederick was elected on March 4 and promptly moved with his family to Philadelphia to take up office, after which he no longer served as an active minister. The next year, he was elected a member of the Pennsylvania Assembly and served as Speaker through 1783. In December 1781, he purchased the house adjacent to his father's and moved there early the following year (figs. 2.10 and 2.11). True to Kuntze's remarks, however, he soon went into business as well. Although wealth was not guaranteed by becoming a merchant, doing so did create an opportunity to acquire it. In addition, Frederick's in-laws, the Schaeffers, had long been engaged in sugar refining and the import business. In April 1782, Henry noted that carpenters were at work on Frederick's store, where Henry and Mary became frequent patrons, purchasing items such as candles, soap, powdered ink, paper, woolen gloves, mitts, handkerchiefs,

FIGURE 2.10
House of Frederick and Catharine Muhlenberg from 1781–91, built 1763–64 for John Schrack, Trappe, Montgomery County. The mansard roof was added during a c. 1870 remodeling. The Speaker's House, Trappe, Pa.

FIGURE 2.11
Artist's rendering of the house in fig. 2.10 as it appeared c. 1781, by Julie Longacre, 2010. The Speaker's House, Trappe, Pa.

trousers, sewing notions, fabrics, medicines, sugar, salt, coffee, tea, molasses, tobacco, wine and spirits. Frederick settled into life in Trappe as a part-time gentleman farmer and merchant when his political duties allowed. Shortly after his arrival, he wrote to Henry Jr., "And now brother, I enjoy my life, indeed by the sweat of my brow, but still faraway from the turmoil of the city, and of the unquiet political life. Here no clients and petitioners plague me," he continued, "nor hundreds of other inquisitive researchers, who at my house in the city continually swarmed, but rather I can delete my work in the garden, in the field, and in the store leisurely wait on [customers], and my constitution begins to get stronger in this healthy air." The property was later described in 1801 as including "a genteel convenient Dwelling House, Store-house, Stone Barn, Carriage-House, Waggon-house, Milk-house, and Smoke-house, with Pump near the Kitchen Door."[18]

While Frederick's political star was rising, Peter went on to serve with distinction during the war. After he helped to defend a British attack on Charleston, South Carolina, Peter was appointed to brigadier general in 1777. At the battle of the Brandywine, his brigade slowed the momentum of the British advance long enough for the bulk of the Continental army to escape and then assisted Anthony Wayne's brigade at Chadds Ford. Two days after the battle of Germantown, in October 1777, Peter offered a twenty-dollar reward for the return of his brass-barreled pistols (fig. 2.12), which he evidently recovered, as thirty years later he bequeathed them to his son Peter Jr., along with his "gold watch marked P.M" (fig. 2.13). Peter suffered through the winter of 1777–78 at Valley Forge, where the reconstructed log huts seen today are on the site of his brigade's encampment. He played a key role in supporting Wayne's assault at the battle of Stony Point and then was sent to Virginia to raise another army for a southern campaign. In 1781, he commanded the brigade that took Redoubt 10 from Cornwallis in the siege at Yorktown. Peter was promoted to major general on September 30, 1783, and retired from the army on November 3 (fig. 2.14).[19] Sometime during or shortly after the war, Peter acquired a second pair of pistols, which he bequeathed to his son Henry and described in his will as "the silver Mounted pistols I bought from General Procter known by the name of Proctors Pistols" (fig. 2.15). The pistols bear the initials "T P" engraved on the thumbpiece, for Thomas Proctor (1739–1806), an Irish immigrant who served as an artillery captain during the Revolution.[20] Proctor resigned from the military in 1781 over a dispute as to whether his artillery unit was under the command of the Continental army or State of Pennsylvania, which may have been when he sold the pistols to Muhlenberg.[21] Evidently Peter had acquired them by February of 1784, when he set out to survey twelve thousand acres of land in western Pennsylvania and the Ohio Territory he had been given in payment for his military service. In his description of the trip, Peter wrote "I have at present the perfect resemblance of Robinson Crusoe: four belts around me, two brace of pistols, a sword and rifle slung, besides my pouch and tobacco-pipe, which is not a small one. . . . I am sure that my appearance alone ought to protect me from both politics and insult."[22]

With both Peter and Frederick having now left the ministry, Henry turned to his youngest son, Henry Jr., to express his concerns. "Poor Peter and Friedrich make me worry my heart out! Oh, how useless, how fleeting are the fortunes of war," he wrote in September 1780.[23] Word from Frederick of his political doings and a possible promotion for Peter in December of that year caused Henry to remark, "You poor worms will climb up higher and higher so that your fall may be all the greater." Given his own aversion to politics, Henry was not surprisingly disturbed by Frederick's political career from the beginning. In November of 1780, he "learned with dismay that *vox populi*, *per plurima vota*, had elected my son Fr[iedrich] Aug[ustus] a member of the state government, and that the Assembly had even chosen him chairman after having served for two years in [the Continental] Congress." Muhlenberg dashed off a letter to warn Frederick that "if he did not by penitent supplication obtain from on high an extraordinary wisdom, a terrible crash and fall would result." In January 1783, Henry received a letter from Frederick, "the contents of which grieved me." "Since he has buried the talent entrusted to him in the political dunghill, the consequences are not lacking." He

FIGURE 2.12
Pair of pistols, owned by Peter Muhlenberg, England, c. 1770–75. Walnut; brass, iron, steel. American Revolution Center

FIGURE 2.13
Pocketwatch, owned by Peter Muhlenberg, probably England, c. 1800. Collection of a descendant

continued, "There has been no lack of warnings, but inquisitive youth prefers to grow wise through its own hurt. But someday he may be utterly consumed with terrors if he does not turn back in time." Part of Henry's concern may have been that Frederick's decision to enter politics would reflect poorly on himself. Henry arranged for Frederick's name be kept out of financial records regarding

FIGURE 2.14
Portrait miniature of Peter Muhlenberg (1746–1807), probably Pennsylvania, c. 1785. Watercolor on ivory. This portrait was painted after Peter's promotion to major general at the end of the war as indicated by the two stars on his epaulettes. Collection of a descendant

FIGURE 2.15
Pair of pistols, owned by Thomas Proctor and then Peter Muhlenberg, Germany and Pennsylvania, c. 1775–85. Stocks of American black walnut, locks marked "Morrow & Welsh" for Abraham Morrow and James Welsh of Philadelphia, and barrels marked "JOH. AND. KUCHENREUTER" for Johann Andreas Kuchenreuter (1716–95) of Steinweg near Regensberg, Bavaria, Germany. Private collection; photo courtesy of Winterthur Museum

the distribution of a church legacy from Germany for fear that his benefactors might conclude "that it was with my consent that my son had given up his ministry." On learning that Frederick had been elected president of the Council of Censors in Philadelphia and also justice of the peace, Henry wrote, "Poor worm! Your downfall is nigh!" In September 1783, Henry's worst fears were nearly confirmed. Militia troops shot and killed Moses Doane, a member of the infamous Doane gang, and imprisoned Joseph Doane in Philadelphia. A note was found on Moses' body threatening to "put Mulinburgh to Death in ten Days without fail" if Joseph was not released from prison and acquitted. As a result of the threat, Frederick Muhlenberg was escorted by a sheriff and three colonels when he traveled from Philadelphia to Trappe on September 6. His father wrote fearfully, "The purpose of the gang is to kidnap the speaker of the Assembly or the governor of the Council.... And since Fr M is still speaker of the Assembly and visits his family in Providence on Saturdays," he added, "some of the gang who live not far away consider him the nearest object which they might most easily seize.... Without God's protection his house and barn are not safe for a single night." Fortunately Frederick was spared any physical harm, but the incident only confirmed his father's opinion that politics was a dangerous game.[24]

Failing to persuade Frederick to return to the ministry, Henry then tried to convince him and his brother Peter that they should become farmers. In February 1785, he warned them, "It is futile to expect a public office here in the country, for there are too many hungry pretenders and parties." "Under such circumstances," he continued, "I should not wish my worst enemy to be an officeholder." He also discouraged their being merchants, writing that "anyone who wishes to support himself and his family in these times by keeping a store or a shop . . . must have the eyes of a falcon, the alertness of a rooster, the fluency of a Jew, the patience of a mule," in addition to enduring unremarkable profits, the expense of employing a clerk, and the constant risk of theft. "According to my humble opinion," he continued, the "most innocent way of living is still the patriarchal way. . . . If you my two dear older sons would have such country places where you could cultivate the soil and raise cattle, where you bring up your children in true Christianity, and . . . give them a good example of Christian conduct, you would provide yourselves with a pleasant and comfortable evening of your lives." Finally, he added, "If you do not act as is fitting for ordinary Christians to act, you will come to a terrible end. . . . Our transient political independence does not free us for a moment . . . from the dependence and the duties which we owe to God, our Redeemer, our neighbors, and ourselves."[25]

FIGURE 3.1
Detail of portrait of Frederick Augustus Muhlenberg in fig. 3.15. National Portrait Gallery, Smithsonian Institution

CHAPTER THREE
PATRIARCHS

By the end of the War for Independence, Henry Muhlenberg was in his seventy-third year, and age was beginning to take its toll. "The tabernacle is becoming more and more dilapidated," he remarked in 1777. The following year, he went temporarily deaf due to the loud report of guns at a military funeral and suffered from permanent hearing loss. "My deafness," he wrote, "detracts from the delight of conversation because I cannot understand softly spoken words, and loud speech sounds more like angry quarreling and displeasure. . . . Nor can anyone speak to me privately of some secret matter without being heard at a distance." After a dinner with several friends, he lamented, "On such occasions I feel very acutely my lack of hearing, and it is a grief to me, because I must sit in silence and cannot join the conversation or speak more intimately to the heart." As the problem grew worse, Henry came to rely on his son Frederick (fig. 3.1) to speak on his behalf with visitors and then communicate with him by writing, as Henry could no longer "confer with him orally on account of my want of hearing." In April 1782, Mary wrote to their daughter Elisabeth that Henry had decided "to show them the kind of old hero he still was" by trying to mount his horse without a mounting block. After three failed attempts, he finally led the horse to the block and got on. "Had he listened to me, he would have stayed home," she added. On another occasion, Henry "dragged" himself to Augustus to preach and afterwards "was weak and tired and preferred to go home through the woods instead of on the open highway. I tried to leap over a ditch, but came short and fell in, so that I had to wash myself before I was able to hobble on home." "The spirit is willing," he concluded, "but the flesh is weak." To help save his strength while preaching, he had a folding seat installed in the pulpit of Augustus Lutheran Church (fig. 3.2).[1]

FIGURE 3.2
Folding seat in pulpit of Augustus Lutheran Church, Trappe, Montgomery County.

Mary, despite being seventeen years younger than Henry, was in declining health. By 1767 she began to suffer from what Henry referred to variously as fits, seizures, or severe epileptic paroxysms. The illness had a profound impact on her quality of life. Of the six letters that survive in Mary's hand, all mention her illness in some way. Two are signed "your miserable mother," one "your sick mother," and one "your miserable wife." Mary tried countless medicines and remedies, ranging from a "mixture of molten sulphur and steel" to keeping a "pair of turtledoves in her bedroom to draw her sickness to them." In 1774, Henry noted, "My wife's attacks, which are occurring frequently these days, are added to my other cares and troubles." He pitied "my friends whenever I am forced to leave my ailing wife in their care because they are always more frightened by her seizures than I am, since I am more accustomed to them." Five years later Mary confided to their daughter Elisabeth, "We need each other now more than ever. He would not get along well without me, and I—hopeless without him."[2] In February 1781, Mary came close to death after a horrific accident caused by a seizure. Henry's unforgettable account of the incident reveals not only her suffering but also the depths of his concern and affection for her:

> In the afternoon I had a visit from a neighbor who had all sorts of things to relate. My wife was with us and, feeling some symptoms of her illness, she went out into the kitchen. A kettle of red beets was hanging over the fire cooking, and she sat down on a small bench near it. Just then she was seized with a *paroxismus epil[epticus]* and she fell into the boiling pot with her left hand, breast, shoulder, right arm, neck, and half of her face. Immediately afterward she came back where I was, trembling, shivering, and wet. I was horrified and called our children at once. We put her to bed, and after she had regained consciousness she felt unspeakable pain from the burns she had suffered in the places aforementioned. My daughter, Mrs. Sw[aine], hastily ground up some potatoes, soaked them in sweet oil, and made poultices in hope of killing the burn. We also sent a neighbor seven miles to fetch a well-known English doctor. The neighbor came back late without having accomplished his purpose because he had not been able to get across the swollen Perkiomen River. The injury was severe, and there is danger in delay. Not only the outer but the second layer of skin and muscles were burned. I had prescriptions but no ingredients. It was a distressing night we put in. A neighbor who has some knowledge of chemistry made up a salve for burns according to Dr. Tissot's prescription, but the swelling and inflammation increased. The patient had read in the church history several days before about the terrible tortures of the first Christians, which served to strengthen her in her pain.

Their daughter Mary Swaine and several neighboring women spent the next weeks in constant attendance on Mary, with Henry hovering anxiously about. The pain Mary suffered was almost unbearable, preventing her from getting any sleep for an entire week. Her recovery was further complicated by her illness, which caused her to have more seizures and tear open the healing wounds. On March 13, Henry reported that her hand and arm were healed, but the burns on the breast, chin, neck, cheeks, and ears were still raw and had to be bandaged twice a day. The first mention of her being out of bed was nearly three months after the accident, when Henry reported that she had another seizure while standing by the door of the house, "which caused the unhealed wounds of her burns to be injured afresh." Mary ultimately recovered from the accident sufficiently enough to resume household activities but continued to have seizures. Henry keenly felt both of their infirmities, observing one day, "We two old folks had a miserable night; she had several violent epileptic paroxysms and I had a catarrhal fever and fits of coughing." When Mary suffered an attack in June 1783, Henry was unable to help her: "Spent the day doing some writing, reading, and worrying. My poor wife fell to the floor in a severe *paroxismus*. I was alone and had to let her lie until she came to again." On another occasion, he "tried to help her to her armchair but was too weak and fell to the floor with her."[3]

On June 12, 1784, Henry received word from son-in-law John Christopher Kuntze that Henry had been awarded an honorary doctor of divinity degree from the University of Pennsylvania. "Dearest Father," Kuntze wrote, "It is with a truly profound feeling of joy that I desire to congratulate you upon receiving the doctor's degree, though I can imagine the expression on your face when you received it." Henry's self-deprecating reply noted that "the D.D. in the address so frightened me that I opened the letter with trembling, since I knew nothing about it previously." Henry recalled that when he first immigrated to America, "I was called 'Doctor' because I wore a gown and a plaited rose on my hat and had some Halle medicines to give away," and continued,

> but now all that has ceased and the highly learned, wise, and estimable trustees of a world famous university ought properly to be more prudent and thrifty and grant their doctor of divinity degrees only to worthy candidates . . . and not waste them on an old, decrepit, deaf, lame, and unlearned Mühlenberg who . . . does not consider himself worthy to be called an accomplished catechist, driller, or preacher, much less a D.D.[4]

Although Muhlenberg went on to protest "this unmerited title," it was probably on this occasion that his portrait was painted by Charles Willson Peale, who depicted Henry in clerical attire, holding a book with a large column in the background (fig. 3.3).[5] Within weeks of receiving notice of the award, Henry noted in his journal that he had "received my old ministerial clothing from Philadelphia," possibly in preparation for sitting for his portrait. A miniature that depicts a similar image is framed in a double-sided locket together with a miniature of Peter Muhlenberg (see fig. 2.14) and descended in his line of the family (fig. 3.4).[6] No portrait of Mary Muhlenberg is known to exist, possibly because of the accident in 1781 in which she severely scalded "half of her face." It took more than five months for her to recover and may have left her face permanently scarred.[7]

FIGURE 3.3
Portrait of Henry Melchior Muhlenberg, engraved by James W. Steel after Charles Willson Peale (1741–1827), from William B. Sprague, *Annals of the American Pulpit; or Commemorative Notices of Distinguished American Clergymen of Various Denominations,* vol. 9 (New York: Robert Carter & Brothers, 1869), frontispiece. Krauth Memorial Library, Lutheran Theological Seminary at Philadelphia

FIGURE 3.4
Portrait miniature of Henry Melchior Muhlenberg, probably Pennsylvania, c. 1785. Watercolor on ivory. Collection of a descendant

Henry became increasingly sentimental as he grew older. In September 1783, he commented, "My flattering egotism builds upon the fantasy that my chaffy journal . . . contained a few grains of wheat and might have given some pleasure and edification to my God-fearing friends in Europe and numerous descendants here in America. . . . [It] can be examined by one or another of my descendants, if they think it worth the while and have time to do so." The same year he "looked through my so-called *Stambüchlein* in which were written, for memory's sake, the names of former prominent and lesser Christian friends, relatives, and patrons in Europe from 1735 to 1742. The great majority of them are now before the throne of the Lamb of God." Four years later, he looked through the album (fig. 3.5) once again and read "the excellent greetings, admonitions, and consolations which various counts, barons, citizens, theologians, etc. inscribed between 1735 and 1742. I suppose that most, if not all, of these blessed persons have died before 1787. . . . Meanwhile I, wretched man that I am, remain here." On Easter Sunday in 1786, Henry wrote, "In the afternoon my wife persuaded me to crawl with her once again, and perhaps for the last time, to the home of our son Fr[ederick]

Aug[ustus]. He gathered his wife and seven children about him and together they played and sang several edifying hymns." The convenient location of Frederick's house next to his parents provided a natural gathering point for the family as well as additional lodging. When out-of-town family members visited, Henry described the situation as "swarming, scrambling, and uproar in our and Fr[ederick] M[uhlenberg's] house." In 1787, Henry presented four of his grandchildren with copies of the recently published Lutheran hymnal (fig. 3.6), for which he had written the preface and assisted in the selection of hymns. When Frederick's wife brought the children over to visit, Henry "wrote some verses" in their hymnals.[8]

In the fall of 1785, Muhlenberg fell ill for almost two weeks with fever and chills. "My children," he wrote—including Peter, Frederick, and Sally—"visited me diligently, and I was nursed, waited upon, and moved about day and night by my daughter Mary Sw[aine]." On February 3, 1787, Henry reported that he had "signed the agreement between me and my son, John Peter, concerning the sale of our home, etc. My wife is much troubled with hysterical fits and desires to be released." Prompted by age and infirmities, the elder Muhlenbergs had decided to sell the property to Peter and his wife, Hannah. According to the agreement, they would continue living there and be provided with "food, drink, and laundry" for £2.10 a month in addition to "an additional £10 for a maid's wages." In preparation for the transition, Henry wrote that "we two old sick people cleared out our living room and moved into the smaller room." Before Peter had even moved in, he began updating the house to his liking. On April 27, he "sent up a mechanicum to strip the walls of our rooms and cover them with paper." Henry, who was put off by all the commotion, complained that "this causes considerable disturbance because the household has not yet been brought into order and we two oldsters and the two small children increase the disorder." Peter's remodeling of the house continued into July. On July 4, Henry noted, "Today Mr. Kugler ripped down the front porch on the *ordre* of G[eneral] P[eter] M[ühlenberg]." The following two days a carpenter and mason were there to build "a new front porch and the

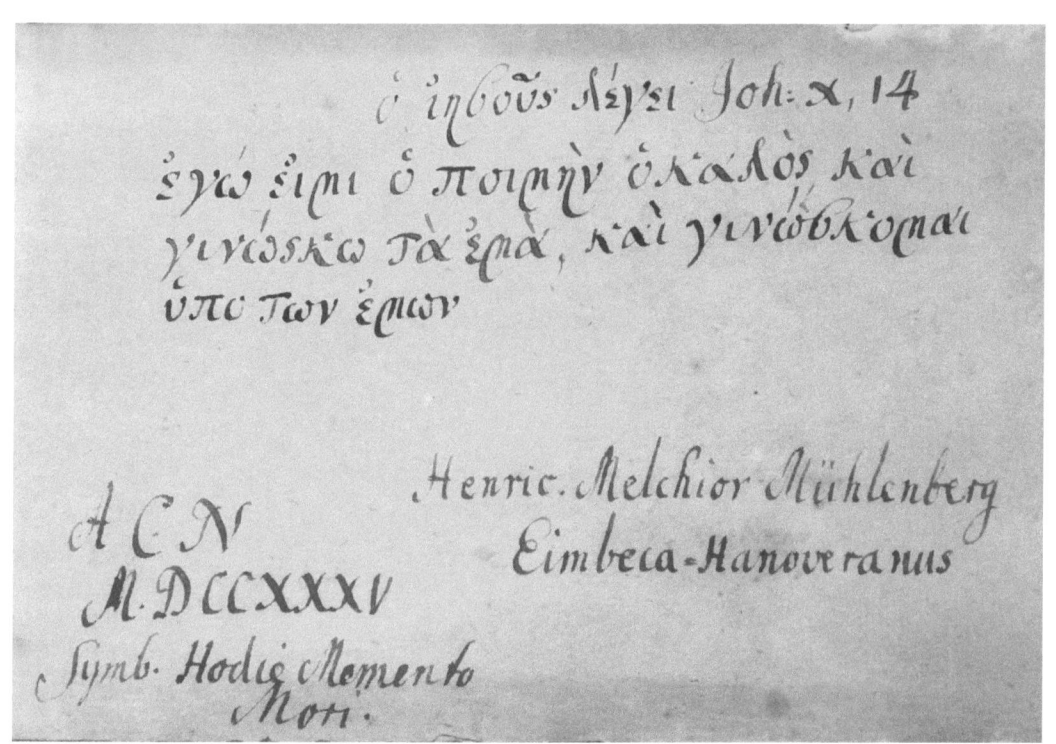

FIGURE 3.5
Signature album, owned by Henry Melchior Muhlenberg, c. 1740. Lutheran Archives Center, Lutheran Theological Seminary at Philadelphia

FIGURE 3.6
Erbauliche Lieder-Samlung Zum Gottesdienstlichen Gebrauch in den Vereinigten Evangelisch Lutherischen Gemeinen in Nord-America (Germantown: Peter Leibert and Michael Billmeyer, 1786). Krauth Memorial Library, Lutheran Theological Seminary at Philadelphia

scaffolding for the wall." "Meanwhile," Henry added, "the painter is painting inside our house," and the walls were whitewashed "in order to get rid of the insects which have gained the upper hand there."[9]

Peter Muhlenberg's actions to update the physical appearance of the house reflected the tastes and sensibilities of his generation and caused Henry some concern, but not nearly so much as the modern behaviors he soon observed in his son's family. On June 27, he wrote disapprovingly that "today Mrs. Hanna had a first visit at her table from several neighboring women according to the prevailing fashion. They drink a glass of wine or a cup of tea and some cakes in the afternoon and evening and entertain one another with vain conversation. This fashion," he warned, "is not according to the counsel and command of our Lord. . . . If poverty and need come as a consequence, such table companions will remain far off." Henry associated fashionable tastes with the younger generation and again voiced his disapproval, writing, "If one considers old and young Americans in general from a purely philosophical point of view, they [the young Americans] concentrate all the senses upon the tongue, or, in other words, upon refined taste." He wrote admiringly of country people who came to church in their working clothes, noting they looked "much superior to the stiff and foolish garments of fashion." In regard to his own appearance, Henry remarked, "It would strike a learned man, brought up in the civilized taste of Europe, as strange to see such a rough, bent, decrepit bungler like myself, especially because I have forgotten all the French compliments, overtures, obeisances, and other dislocations of one's limbs." On another occasion, after receiving a pair of breeches from Peter as a gift, he noted, "I cannot present the figure of a gentleman in them and am happy if I can cover my nakedness."[10]

Henry also disapproved of the manner in which Peter's children were being reared. In June 1787, he gave his grandson "some blows with a rod because he came home late, etc., whereupon he threatened to remain out late again tomorrow evening to play." Perhaps Henry recalled an incident many years earlier when he "punished Peter, who went out without permission and did not come home until about nine o'clock." A firm believer in physical discipline, Henry commented that "if parents do not in time break the inborn, selfish wickedness and self-will which are inherited from Adam," children "will become thorns, etc. in their sides." To this he added, "the pushing of a barrow in Philadelphia, the pillory, the gallows, or all sorts of incurable diseases will occur as consequences of their unbridled sins, etc."[11] Three years earlier, Henry expressed his views on the subject in a letter to his youngest son, Henry Jr., in Lancaster. On hearing that two of the Schultzes' children were sickly, Henry said "The trouble is not with their bodies but with their unbroken and spoiled willfulness." "I cannot approve," he bemoaned, "the way they bring up children here. . . . Instead of being brought up to be of use to the common weal, they are brought up to crime. . . . Instead of dieting," he went on, "children are stuffed all day long like young pigs or geese. . . . If the parents say to one of these children 'come,' he goes; 'go,' and he comes, 'do this' and he does the opposite." He concluded by noting, "I don't have to go far for an example of bad bringing up, as within a few weeks I have observed Joh[an] Pet[er']s three offshoots, before that M[iste]r Sch[ultze]'s three grown up children . . . also Fr[ederick]'s five children."[12]

In 1785, Henry complained of "poor sight, deafness, swollen feet, constant dizziness in the head, trembling in all my members, etc. [which] prevent me from dressing and undressing, walking and standing, etc. without help." Several years prior, after preparing his last will and testament, he commented, "When a man enters the seventies he, above all, may well sing, 'Who knoweth how near is my end?'"[13] Though the will did not contain any special bequests of objects, in a letter to Henry Jr. he wrote that his son was to receive "the small distilling kettle" and his "Hebrew Bible in folio" after his death (figs. 3.7 and 3.8).[14] Sensing that his time was nearing, Henry made special efforts in 1787 to visit his children and grandchildren. In April he wrote, "Together with my sick wife I crawled once more to the home of my son, Fr[ederick] Aug[ustus]." In May, Frederick brought word that his father-in-law, David Schaeffer, had passed away, causing Henry to remark that "one after another, my old friends are departing,

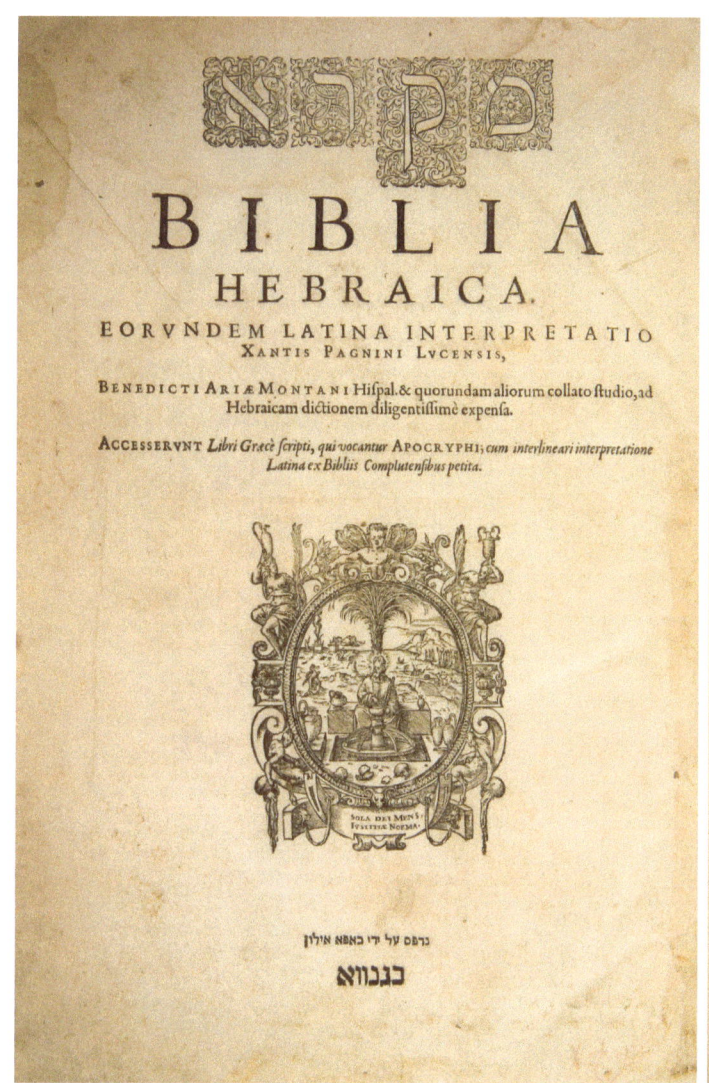
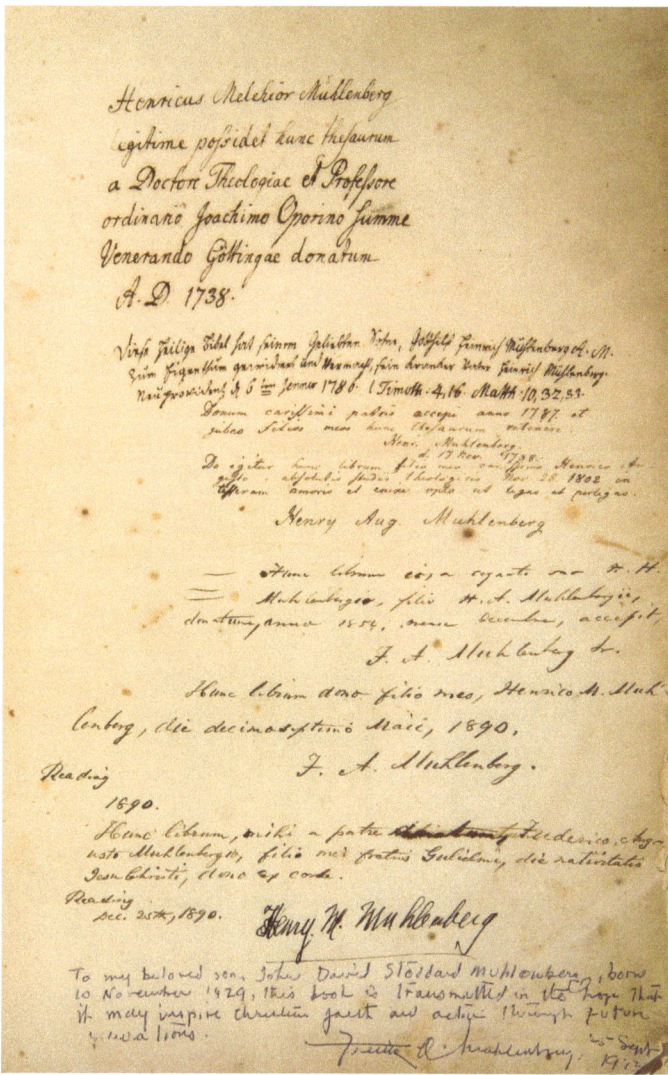

and I must remain behind as a stranger." In July, Henry and Mary spent ten days with the Swaines in New Hanover while the Trappe house was being renovated. On the day of their departure he wrote that "with great effort, my children lifted me into the wagon, where bedding had been prepared, and drove me, with my sick wife and daughter, to New Hanover." By mid-August, Henry's journal entries became increasingly shorter and less frequent. On August 19 he observed that "my weaknesses of body and mind are increasing." His final journal entry was made on Saturday, September 29. Befitting his long career as a minister, it read: "Baptized Anna, infant daughter of Joh. Frey and his wife Hanna. The child was 15 months old. The parents were sponsors."

The following Sunday, October 7, 1787, Henry Melchior Muhlenberg drew his last breath. His funeral was held on October 10 at Augustus Lutheran Church, where so many people gathered that the service had to be delivered outdoors. Henry was laid to rest along the exterior wall of the church in the nearest position to the pulpit that he had occupied since the construction of the church in 1743. A six-foot-long marble slab (fig. 3.9) erected over his grave bears a lengthy Latin inscription memorializing his life and deeds, concluding with the phrase "who and what he was future ages will know without a stone." Mary lived another fifteen years and died on August 23, 1802. She was buried next to Henry, as noted on the tombstone, which reads, "Here are also

FIGURES 3.7 and 3.8
Biblia Hebraica, owned by Henry Melchior Muhlenberg. Inscriptions record the transfer of the Bible from Henry Melchior Muhlenberg to his son Henry Muhlenberg Jr., then to his son Henry Augustus Muhlenberg, to his son Hiester Henry Muhlenberg, to Frederick Augustus Muhlenberg Sr., to Frederick Augustus Muhlenberg Jr., to his son John D. S. Muhlenberg. Collection of a descendant

deposited the Remains of Anna Maria Muhlenberg." A lengthy *Denkmal*, or memoriam, was published after Henry's death, containing more than sixty pages of hymns, poems, and tributes (fig. 3.10). Three years prior to Henry's death, his son-in-law, Christopher Kuntze, told him, "Dearest Father . . . Your memory will never die in America, and I hope that posterity will read much concerning you."[15] In recognition of his forty-five years of devoted ministry, Henry Melchior Muhlenberg became known as the patriarch of the Lutheran Church in America. He was also the patriarch of one of the most influential Pennsylvania German families in history, whose members would make their own important contributions.

No inventory was taken when Henry Muhlenberg died in 1787, and few objects survive that can be definitively associated with him. A glass mug with engraved floral decoration and a silver lid engraved with his initials, "H M," was carefully preserved by his descendants and may have been brought with him from Europe or later imported

FIGURE 3.9
Tombstone of Henry Melchior Muhlenberg and Anna Maria Weiser Muhlenberg at Augustus Lutheran Church, Trappe, Montgomery County.

FIGURE 3.10
Denkmal der Liebe und Achtung . . . dem Herrn D. Heinrich Melchior Mühlenberg (Philadelphia: Melchior Steiner, 1788). Collection of a descendant

(fig. 3.11). A decanter and set of five wineglasses that have also been associated with him could date as early as 1785 (fig. 3.12). With their engraved neoclassical motifs—including swags, bowknots, and husks—the glassware would have been fashionable for his children's generation as well.[16] References to seating furniture appear throughout Henry's journals, including the set of "new chairs" he bought in 1763 (see fig. 1.24), another set of six chairs purchased in 1771, an armchair, two caned chairs, and a commode or pot chair. Henry also owned a "couch" or daybed and a writing desk, in which he stored his vast correspondence and other documents. Numerous cooking implements and tableware are mentioned, including "twelve plates and a sugar bowl of white porcelain," wineglasses, and "large brass candlesticks." Extensive pewter is also listed, including six plates, two shallow platters, a porringer, and two tankards. The few personal items that Henry notes include a pocket watch, shaving mirror, and snuff box (fig. 3.13).[17]

After Henry's death, Frederick and Peter continued to advance in their careers. When Frederick

FIGURE 3.11
Mug, owned by Henry Melchior Muhlenberg, probably Bohemia, c. 1750–75. Glass; silver. Lutheran Archives Center, Lutheran Theological Seminary at Philadelphia

FIGURE 3.12
Decanter and set of five wineglasses, descended in the Muhlenberg family, England or America, c. 1785–1800. Glass. Lutheran Archives Center, Lutheran Theological Seminary at Philadelphia

FIGURE 3.13
Snuff box, owned by Henry Melchior Muhlenberg, probably Pennsylvania, c. 1775. Silver. Marked three times on the underside "L H" within a rectangular surround. Martin Art Gallery, Muhlenberg College, Allentown, Pa., presented by Rev. J. W. Bittner, class of 1907

FIGURE 3.14

FEDERAL HALL: The Seat of CONGRESS, printed and engraved by Amos Doolittle (1754–1832) after a drawing by Pierre Lacour (New Haven, Conn.: Amos Doolittle, 1790). Winterthur Museum, 1957.816

moved back to Trappe in 1782, he was then serving a second term as Speaker of the Pennsylvania Assembly. In 1784, he was elected register of wills and recorder of deeds for the newly formed Montgomery County. The same year, Peter was elected to the Supreme Executive Council of Pennsylvania and served as vice president under Benjamin Franklin through 1788. Three years later, Frederick was president of the Pennsylvania Constitutional Convention. On November 26, 1788, Frederick and Peter were elected to the United States House of Representatives. They traveled to New York in March 1789 and waited for enough delegates to form a quorum. Frederick wrote to his friend Dr. Benjamin Rush in Philadelphia,

> My friends here . . . think of me as a Candidate for the Speakers Chair. . . . Never did I dread a Business more, & I feel the want of Abilities & knowledge to such a Degree that the Thought of it makes me tremble & yet on the other Hand to refuse . . . those who have honoured me with their Confidence & a Seat in the Legislature would in my opinion be a Crime which I hope never to be guilty of.

On April 4, Frederick was elected Speaker by a vote of 23–7. The *Pennsylvania Packet* announced, "the German gentleman has been honored with the chair of speaker of the legislature" while the *Philadelphische Correspondenz* proclaimed that "the blood of the grandchildren of our grandchildren will proudly well up in their hearts when they will read in the histories of America that the first Speaker . . . was a German, born of German parents in Pennsylvania." This sense of pride resulted in Frederick's election as president of the German Society of Pennsylvania in 1790, a position which he held until 1797. The speakership was modeled on the British House of Commons and was intended as an office of high honor. The salary, twelve dollars a day, was twice that of regular congressmen because of the level of entertaining that was expected. "I sincerely confess," Frederick wrote to Rush, "that I would rather have had a less Sum & not be under the Necessity of keeping up that Form & parade which is now in some Measure expected & which I ever had a natural Aversion to."[18] Despite such claims of modesty, evidence suggests that Frederick and Peter filled their free time in New York with a whirlwind of social activities, including dinners with President Washington, afternoon teas and levies, and travels about the city in Frederick's carriage. Both were present for Washington's inauguration on April 30, 1789, on the balcony of Federal Hall, the seat of the First Congress (fig. 3.14). As Speaker, Frederick hosted a weekly gathering of the Pennsylvania congressmen. William Maclay (1737–1804), a senator from Pennsylvania, described these dinners as affairs of excessive drinking, smoking, and base conversation. In July 1789, Maclay wrote, "I had been pressed to dine with the Speaker in a Company of Pennsylvanians . . . I came away quite tired of the volatile Tattle of the Table, I never had much but now much less taste, for convivial Joy." The following May, he noted, "And this being club day, I went to dine, with the

Pennsylvania mess[.] We sat down to dinner half after 3[.] eating stopped our mouths Untill about 4 & from that to near 9 I never heard such a Scene of Beastial Ba[w]dry kept up in my life." In May 1790, Maclay noted, "I have drank Wine with the Speaker at the rate of about 3 Glasses [per] day and I really consider myself Worse for it."[19]

In July 1790, Frederick had his portrait painted by Joseph Wright (fig. 3.15). The painting shows Frederick seated in a distinctive settee, one of two commissioned for Federal Hall.[20] The *Columbian Magazine* observed of Muhlenberg that "his portly person and handsome rotundity, literally filled the chair. His rubicund complexion and oval face," the article continued, "hair full powdered, tamboured satin vest of ample dimensions, dark blue coat with gilt buttons, and a sonorous voice . . . all corresponding in appearance and sound with his magnificent name." Frederick is depicted in the act of signing several documents, one of them being House Bill no. 65, *An Act to Regulate Trade and Intercourse with the Indian Tribes*.[21] A

FIGURE 3.15
Portrait of Frederick Augustus Conrad Muhlenberg, by Joseph Wright (1756–93), New York, 1790. Oil on canvas with applied wood strip. National Portrait Gallery, Smithsonian Institution

FIGURE 3.16
Portrait of Catharine Schaeffer Muhlenberg, attributed to Joseph Wright (1756–93), probably New York, c. 1790. Whereabouts unknown; reproduced from Henrietta Meier Oakley and John Christopher Schwab, *Muhlenberg Album* (New Haven, Conn.: the authors, 1910).

companion portrait of his wife, Catharine, was probably painted about the same time (fig. 3.16).[22] Following his first term as Speaker, during which time he became the first signer of the Bill of Rights, Frederick served in the next three congresses and was Speaker again during the Third Congress. During the Fourth Congress, there was heated debate over ratification of the Jay Treaty, negotiated by Chief Justice John Jay, to resolve outstanding issues between the United States and England. The treaty was wildly unpopular with many Americans who felt it gave too many concessions to England, though implementation was necessary to give the young nation time to rebuild in preparation for future conflict. After ratification by the Senate, a wave of public outrage erupted in which angry mobs burned John Jay in effigy. The treaty then went to the House, which dissolved into a committee of the whole and selected Frederick Muhlenberg the chairman. The committee's vote was divided evenly, forty-nine for and forty-nine against, leaving Frederick to cast the tie-breaking vote. He opted in favor of the treaty, an action that ended his political career and nearly his life when he was stabbed by his own brother-in-law, Bernhard Schaeffer. Jacob Hiltzheimer of Philadelphia wrote in his diary on May 6, 1796, "Observed a crowd of people on Fifth Street going toward Chestnut, and on inquiring found that the constables were taking Bernard Shaffer to gaol for stabbing his brother-in-law, F. A. Muhlenberg, two days ago. Shaffer dangerously stabbed Constable West when making the arrest."[23] Schaeffer was imprisoned for a year and heavily fined for his actions. Frederick survived but was not re-elected. On January 8, 1800, he was appointed by Pennsylvania Governor Thomas McKean as receiver general of the Land Office. He moved with his family to Lancaster as this was then the state capital.

On June 4, 1801, Frederick died of a stroke at the age of fifty-one. His death, wrote future Secretary of the U.S. Treasury William Duane to President Thomas Jefferson, "has produced a change in the political prospects in this state. His conduct on the British treaty lost him the confidence of all the independent republicans; the opposite party had determined to run him for Governor. . . . There is no other character among the Germans of talents and standing equal to the deceased; his capacity as a German writer was admired, and there does not appear to be any one equal to him left."[24] Frederick died intestate and his widow sold many of their household goods; consequently, few objects remain in the possession of descendants today. Among the most personal items that have been preserved are Frederick's silver snuff box and gold-tipped cane, both engraved with his initials (fig. 3.17). The inventory of his estate, taken on June 18, 1801, reveals that his household was well-equipped for fine dining and entertaining, including a large mahogany dining table with two circular ends, a sideboard, fifty-seven wineglasses, two mahogany knife cases, a tureen, two dozen soup plates, "3 Butter Boats" and "4 Pickle Shells," and eighteen custard cups. The walls were adorned with several looking glasses, one "large picture" and six other "pictures," probably family portraits, as well as a "picture of Washington" and bust of Benjamin Franklin. Other items included a "spinet" valued at £7.10.0, a violin, chessboard, mahogany desk-and-bookcase worth £15, ten mahogany chairs (two arm) and a mahogany sofa, and a gold watch (at £22.10, the most expensive object in the inventory). The inventory listed numerous items of silver as well, including a "plated Fish Knife," four plated coasters, and four plated saltcellars, a plated castor set, and one "Tutany [or paktong] Tea Pot and Stand," sugar tongs, more than two dozen spoons, and a "Silver Sugar Dish" valued at £5.12.6, "Silver Slop Bowl" at £7.10.0, and "Cream Jug" at £3.15.0. The latter three objects are engraved with Frederick and Catharine's initials (fig. 3.18) and were probably made by a Philadelphia silversmith. These few items, in addition to the portrait of Frederick painted in 1790 and several later copies (see fig. 4.27), are the only examples of his household furnishings known to survive.

Peter Muhlenberg was a member of the United States House in the First, Third, and Sixth Congresses and was elected to the Senate in the Seventh Congress. He soon resigned from the Senate, however, to become supervisor of United States customs in the district of Philadelphia. In 1803 he was appointed collector of the port of Philadelphia. In this capacity he had much correspondence with Thomas Jefferson with regard to orders that Jefferson had placed for items such as books, raisins, champagne, and wine. On June 17, 1806, Peter purchased a property along the Schuylkill River near Gray's Ferry. The *Aurora* newspaper noted that "among the Germans, the man most celebrated was General Peter Muhlenberg, who had distinguished revolutionary services to be proud of . . . General Muhlenberg, now in the advance of life, with the resolution of a lion when in danger, and with a highly cultivated mind, displays the simplicity of one unacquainted with human affairs, and unsuspecting of human infirmities." Peter's wife, Hannah, became ill and died in October 1806. Peter died on October 1, 1807, his sixty-first birthday. Following a funeral service at Zion Lutheran Church in Philadelphia, he was buried in Trappe alongside his wife and parents, where his tombstone is inscribed: "He was brave

FIGURE 3.17
Snuff box, owned by Frederick Muhlenberg, by John McMullin (1765–1843), Philadelphia, c. 1790. Silver. Collection of a descendant

FIGURE 3.18
Tea service, owned by Frederick and Catharine Muhlenberg, probably Philadelphia, c. 1790. The five cups in the foreground are illustrated in fig. 3.21. Whereabouts unknown; reproduced from Henrietta Meier Oakley and John Christopher Schwab, *Muhlenberg Album* (New Haven, Conn.: the authors, 1910).

in the field, faithful in the cabinet, honorable in all his transactions, a sincere friend and an honest man."

Peter's will, written in July 1807, left $125 to Augustus Lutheran Church for repairs to the churchyard. His daughter Esther was bequeathed $1,000 "in consideration of her faithful attendance upon her Mother and myself" along with "all the Silver Plate . . . The forte piano, The choice of one Bed with its Appurtenances, one sett of Mahogany Chairs to wit six Common and two arm chairs, The pair of large Looking Glasses, one mahogany Table, the two new Bureaus, the new Clock and all her Mother's wearing apparel." To his son Francis he left $1,000 and "all the remaining part of the Furniture with all my Books and all my Guns." Sons Peter Jr. and Henry were each bequeathed a pair of his pistols (see figs. 2.12 and 2.15). The inventory of Peter's estate included prints of Washington and Jefferson, a pouch and powder horn, two "guns" valued at $16, a pair of saddlebags, and two pairs of holsters. On October 15, 1807, his executors, Francis Swaine and John Graff, advertised a sale of "mahogany dining and card tables, side boards, elegant looking glasses, a well toned Forte Piano, pictures, andirons, shovels and tongs, beds and bedding . . . a handsome carriage and Harness, a new sleigh, three Horses, two Cows . . . with a quantity of articles too tedious to enumerate."[25] Many objects, however, remained in the family, including a punch bowl embellished with patriotic emblems and the slogan "Peace, Plenty, and Independence" that was given to Peter by his army officers (figs. 3.19 and 3.20).[26] A set of five silver camp cups, engraved with Peter's initials, also survive (fig. 3.21).[27] In a codicil to his will, dated September 17, 1807, Peter directed his executors to emancipate a slave named Kitty and also exonerated another black indentured servant named Hannah, aged twenty-three, from two of her five remaining years of service. He was not the only Muhlenberg to own slaves as the 1801 inventory of Frederick's estate included "1 Black Servant" valued at £40, and the administrative papers note the sale of "Negro Cato / Servant" for $80.

The youngest Muhlenberg brother, Henry Jr., was the only one to remain a minister (fig. 3.22). Like his older brothers, however, he, too, found a calling beyond the ministry. In 1787, Henry Jr. became the first principal or president of Franklin College in Lancaster (now Franklin and Marshall). The original trustees include his brother Peter, brother-in-law Emanuel Schultze, and Benjamin Franklin—after whom the college was named. On June 6, Henry Jr. "delivered a judicious and elegant sermon in the German language" for the college's dedicatory address, which was printed in a bilingual German-English booklet (fig. 3.23). He also became a renowned botanist. His interest in the subject dated to at least 1778, when he began a botanical diary to record his observations on plants, and his father wrote that he "desires to have Linnaeus' *Philosophia Botanica* from the city when opportunity presents itself."[28] Fearful that Henry Jr. might change careers, his father admonished him in 1780 that the ministry "will give you infinitely more blessing and reward than all this research into hidden variants and the plants of Linnaeus." Swedish scientist Carl Linnaeus (1707–78) was

FIGURE 3.19
Punch bowl, owned by Peter Muhlenberg, probably Staffordshire or Liverpool, England, c. 1800. Pearlware. Collection of a descendant

FIGURE 3.20
Detail of interior of fig. 3.19.

FIGURE 3.21
Set of five camp cups, owned by Peter Muhlenberg, by Philip Garrett (act. c. 1801–35) and (*center*) Jacob Kucher (act. c. 1802–33), Philadelphia, c. 1805. Silver. Collection of a descendant

FIGURE 3.23
Eine Rede Gehalten den 6ten Juny 1787 bey der Einweihung von der Deutschen Hohen Schule oder Franklin Collegium in Lancaster, von Gotthilf Hen. Mühlenberg (Lancaster: Albrecht and Lahn, 1788). Lutheran Archives Center, Lutheran Theological Seminary at Philadelphia

FIGURE 3.22
Portrait of Henry Muhlenberg Jr., by Jacob Eichholtz (1776–1842), Lancaster, 1811. Oil on canvas. Phillips Museum of Art, Franklin and Marshall College

FIGURE 3.24
Lists of plants compiled by Henry Muhlenberg Jr. Krauth Memorial Library, Lutheran Theological Seminary at Philadelphia

the author of the binomial system of nomenclature (*Genus species*), which would have a profound influence on Henry Jr. despite his father's warning. Between 1780 and 1791, he identified nearly 1,100 different plants within a three-mile radius of Lancaster and began to compile voluminous lists of his observations (fig. 3.24). He named more than 160 species while still others were named in his honor, including a species of white oak (*Quercus mühlenbergii*) as well as the now-endangered bog turtle (*Clemmys mühlenbergii*). In 1785 Henry Jr. was elected a member of the American Philosophical Society, along with James Madison and Joseph Priestley. He presented an outline of his observations on plants in the Lancaster area in July 1785 to the society, followed in 1791 by his *Index Flora Lancastriensis*, in which he identified nearly 1,100 species according to the Linnaean system. A supplemental index in 1796 brought his observations of plants in Lancaster County to nearly 1,380 species. In 1809 Henry Jr. began to compile a catalog of North American plants. Containing some 3,670 species, the study was published in 1813 by William Hamilton of Lancaster under the title *A Catalogue of the Hitherto Known Native and Naturalized Plants of North America* (fig. 3.25). In 1814 Thomas Jefferson wrote Henry Jr. to thank him "for your catalogue of North American plants. It is indeed very copious, and at the same time compendious in its form.... I have had long and much gratification in observing the distinguished part you have borne in making known ... the treasures of our own country and I tender to you the sentiments of my high respect and esteem."[29] Muhlenberg also coauthored a two-volume German-English dictionary, the first printed in America, published in 1812 (fig. 3.26).

Muhlenberg's last major work was a treatise on grasses and reeds, *Descriptio uberior graminum et plantarum calamariarum*, which was published posthumously in 1817 (fig. 3.27). Grasses were one of his particular specialties, and he had more than 320 species of American grasses and reeds in his herbarium by 1811. He corresponded with many noteworthy scientists of his day, including William Bartram, to whom he wrote in 1810,

"Hardly a Day passes but I am in Spirit with You and wander with You Hand in Hand through Your Garden and on the Banks of Schulkil" (fig. 3.28).[30] To Dr. William Baldwin, another fellow botanist, he wrote in 1813, "My little garden in which I cultivate North American plants from other parts, gives me daily some entertainment. But how little can a small garden contain." Henry Jr. died on May 23, 1815. His son, Dr. Frederick Augustus Muhlenberg, who had studied medicine under Dr. Benjamin Rush, wrote to inform his father's friends of the sad news. Dr. Baldwin replied, "May the lovers of Botany, throughout the United States, do honor to his memory by walking in his footsteps . . . the Linnaeus of our Country." "With him has fallen one of the oldest, the strongest pillars . . . of botanick science in America." Another botanist, F. André Michaeux, wrote in the introduction to his 1817 book *North American Sylva* that Henry Jr. was "one of the most learned botanists America has hitherto produced." In his will, dated October 11, 1814, Henry directed half of the estate to his widow and half to be divided among their eight children. No mention was made of his botanical research papers or any personal belongings though two of the objects that can be associated with him are an urn-shaped silver sugar bowl and cream pot engraved with the initials, "HCM," for Henry and Catharine Muhlenberg, and their marriage date of "1774" (fig. 3.29).[31] Following his death, Henry Jr.'s extensive herbarium was purchased by friends and presented to the American Philosophical Society in February 1818. It was later transferred to the Academy of Natural Sciences in Philadelphia, where numerous specimens are now preserved.

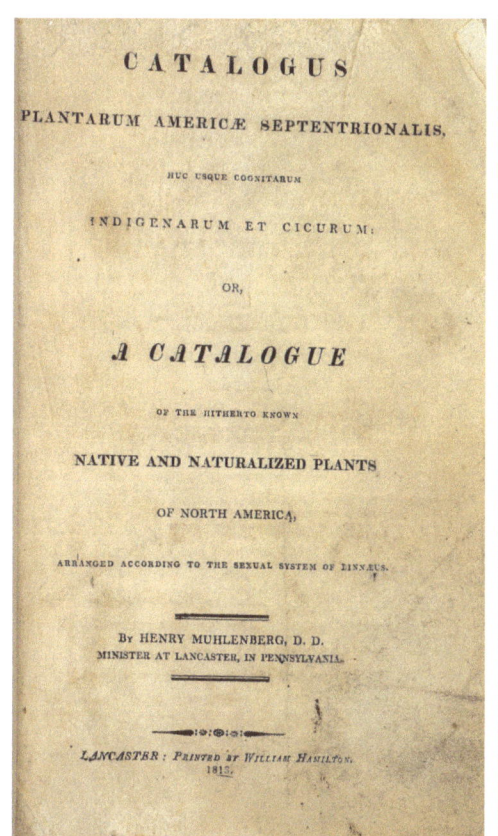

FIGURE 3.25
Henry Muhlenberg Jr., *A Catalogue of the Hitherto Known Native and Naturalized Plants of North America* (Lancaster: William Hamilton, 1813). Winterthur Library, Printed Book and Periodical Collection

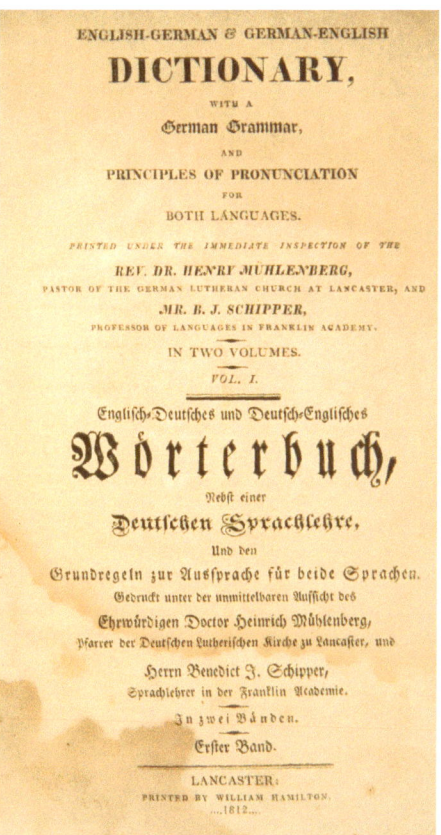

FIGURE 3.26
Henry Muhlenberg Jr., *English-German & German-English Dictionary, with a German Grammar, and Principles of Pronunciation for Both Languages*, 2 vols. (Lancaster: William Hamilton, 1812). Private collection

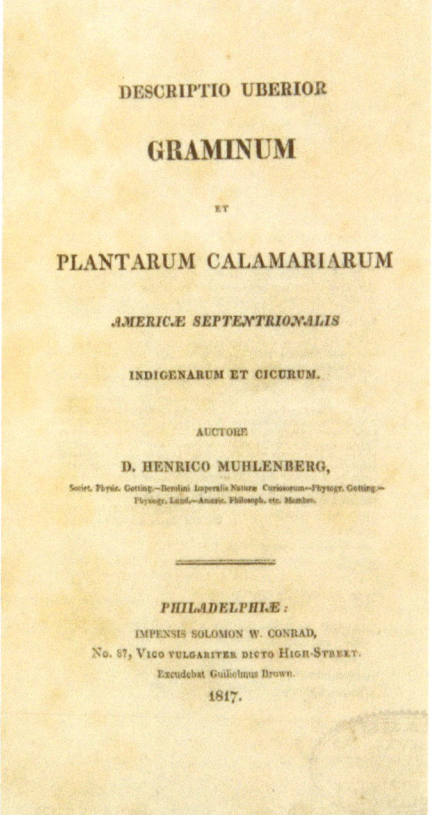

FIGURE 3.27
Henry Muhlenberg Jr., *Descriptio uberior graminum et plantarum calamariarum* (Philadelphia: Solomon W. Conrad, 1817). Krauth Memorial Library, Lutheran Theological Seminary at Philadelphia

FIGURE 3.28
Garden and house of William Bartram, Philadelphia. The Bartrams cultivated rare plants, experimented with hybridization, and harvested seeds that they sold to collectors both in America and abroad from their property along the western banks of the Schuylkill River. John Bartram Association

FIGURE 3.29
Cream pot and sugar bowl, owned by Henry and Catharine Muhlenberg Jr., Philadelphia, c. 1790. Silver. Cream pot: by Joseph and Nathaniel Richardson (1752–1831 and 1754–1827). Collection of the T. Chad Wagner Family. Sugar bowl: by Christian Wiltberger (1766–1851). Collection of the Timothy D. Wagner Family

Conclusion

Subsequent generations of the Muhlenberg family continued to find success in a diverse array of fields, including the ministry, medicine, science, the military, and politics. In recognition of these achievements, numerous places and institutions bear the family name, including Muhlenberg County, Kentucky (est. 1798); Muhlenberg Township, Berks County (est. 1851); and Muhlenberg College (est. 1867) in Allentown, Pennsylvania. Peter Muhlenberg Jr. followed in his father's footsteps and became an army captain during the War of 1812 (fig. 3.30). Two of his great-grandsons achieved particular renown: Dr. Hiester Henry Muhlenberg (1885–1956) as the long-time chief of staff at Reading Hospital and Frederick Augustus Muhlenberg (1887–1980) as a member of the United States House from 1947 to 1949 (figs. 3.31 and 3.32). Frederick Muhlenberg's son David (1784–1849) married Rachel Evans, daughter of Oliver Evans, famed inventor and author of *The Young Mill-wright and Miller's Guide* (1795). In 1815 David Muhlenberg assisted Oliver Evans in making a high-pressured steam engine for the Fairmount Water Works. One of Frederick's grandsons, William Augustus Muhlenberg, became a renowned Episcopal minister and is considered to be the founder of the Episcopal

FIGURE 3.30
Portrait miniature of Peter Muhlenberg Jr. (1787–1844), probably Pennsylvania, c. 1820. Watercolor on ivory. Collection of Brian and Barbara Hendelson

FIGURE 3.31
Medicine bottles, owned by Dr. Hiester Henry Muhlenberg (1885–1956), Reading, Berks County, c. 1925. Private collection

FIGURE 3.32
Campaign buttons of Frederick Augustus Muhlenberg (1887–1980) for the United States House, 1947–49. Private collection

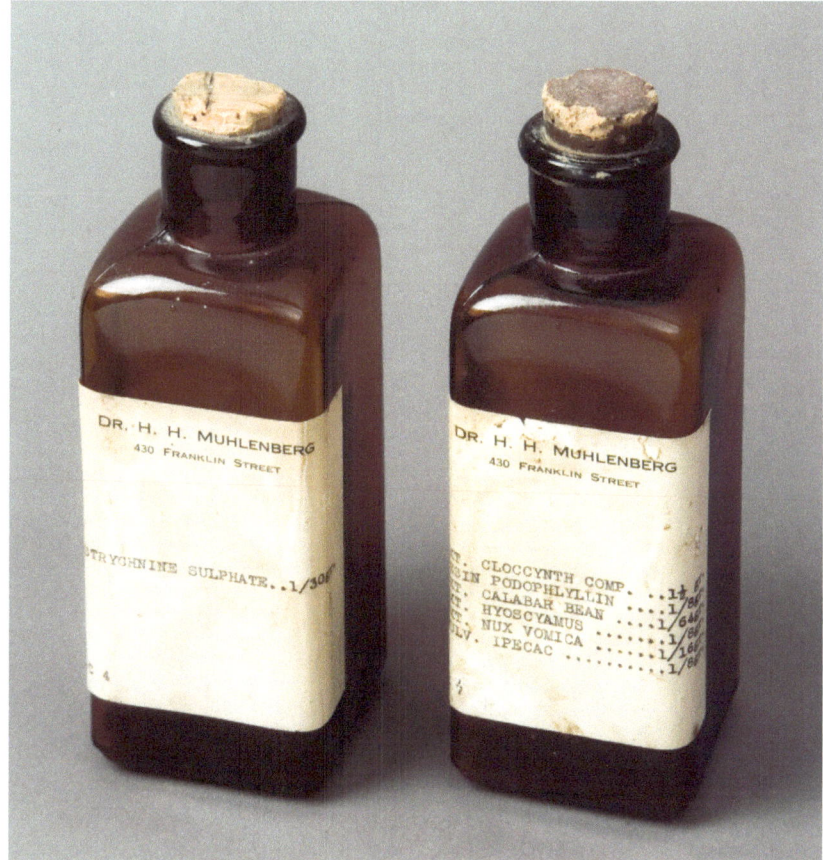

Church School Movement (fig. 3.33). He became headmaster of the Flushing Institute in 1827 and founded St. Luke's Hospital of New York City in 1858.[32] One of Frederick's great-great-grandsons, Edward Brooke (b. 1863), commissioned the renowned architect Frank Furness to design a forty-two-room mansion in Birdsboro, Berks County, that was one of the largest private residences in Pennsylvania at the time of its construction in 1888 (fig. 3.34). Of Henry Muhlenberg Jr.'s children, son Frederick Augustus Hall studied medicine under Benjamin Rush and practiced in Lancaster (fig. 3.35). Another son, Henry Augustus Philip Muhlenberg (1782–1844), was pastor of Trinity Lutheran Church in Reading from 1803 to 1829, United States congressman from 1829 to 1838, and the first United States minister to Austria from 1838 to 1840 (figs. 3.36 and 3.37). He married Mary Elizabeth Hiester, daughter of General Joseph Hiester of Reading (who would later serve as governor of Pennsylvania from 1820 to 1823) and then her sister Rebecca after Mary's death in 1806. Henry Jr.'s grandson, Frederick Augustus Muhlenberg (1818–1901), was a Lutheran minister and the first president of Muhlenberg College. One of Eve Elisabeth Muhlenberg Schultze's sons, John Andrew Melchior, was

Chapter Three: Patriarchs

FIGURE 3.33
Portrait of William Augustus Muhlenberg (1796–1877), probably New York, c. 1850. Oil on canvas. Collection of a descendant

FIGURE 3.34
Brooke mansion, built 1888, photo c. 1925, Birdsboro, Berks County. Collection of a descendant

FIGURE 3.35
Portrait of Dr. Frederick Augustus Hall Muhlenberg (1795–1867), possibly by Jacob Eichholtz (1776–1842), probably Lancaster, c. 1840. Oil on canvas. Christopher T. Rebollo Antiques; photo courtesy of Pook & Pook

FIGURE 3.36
Portrait miniature of Henry Augustus Philip Muhlenberg (1782–1844), by James Peale (1749–1831), Philadelphia, 1806. Watercolor on ivory. Collection of a descendant

FIGURE 3.37
Detail of back of miniature in fig. 3.36.

governor of Pennsylvania from 1823 to 1829 (fig. 3.38). The youngest Muhlenberg daughter, Maria Salome Richards, was the mother of John William Richards (1803–54), a Lutheran minister who served as pastor of Augustus Lutheran Church in Trappe from 1834 to 1836 and as president of the ministerium from 1850 to 1852. His son, Henry Melchior Muhlenberg Richards (1848–1935), was one of the first to study the family history.[33]

Henry Melchior Muhlenberg's decision to accept the call to Pennsylvania in 1741 and his arrival the following year had a profound impact on the development of the Lutheran Church in America as well as on the greater German-speaking community through not only his actions but also those of his descendants, who became important leaders in both church and state affairs (fig. 3.39). On the bicentennial of Henry Melchior Muhlenberg's arrival in 1742, President Franklin Delano Roosevelt issued a statement: "Clergymen, soldiers, scholars, and statesmen, the Muhlenbergs have represented the best in our national life since the earliest days of the Republic."[34] These pastors and patriots continue to live on through their descendants as well as their rich spiritual and material legacy.

FIGURE 3.38
Portrait of John Andrew Melchior Schultze (1775–1852), by Jacob Eichholtz (1776–1842), Lancaster, 1825. Oil on canvas. Philadelphia History Museum at the Atwater Kent, Historical Society of Pennsylvania Collection

FIGURE 3.39
Detail of portrait of Henry Melchior Muhlenberg in fig. 2

APPENDIX A:
GALLERY OF MISSING, UNIDENTIFIED, AND MISCELLANEOUS OBJECTS

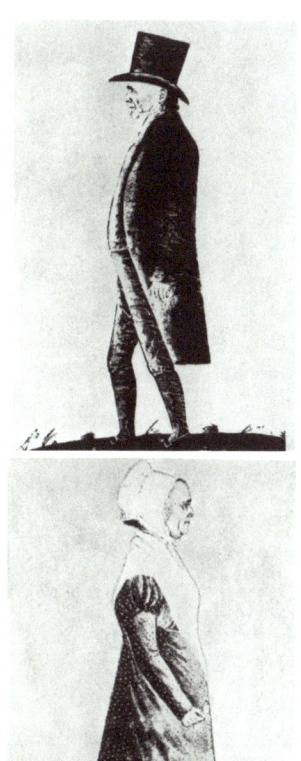

Figs. 4.1 and 4.2. Portraits of unknown man and woman, c. 1730.

Courtesy of the Historical Society of Berks County Museum & Library, Reading, Pa.

This pair of portraits descended in the family of Speaker Frederick Augustus Muhlenberg. Brass plaques on the frames identify them as "Henry Melchior Muhlenberg by John Wollaston 1760" and "Anna Eve Weiser/Daughter of Conrad Weiser & Wife of Henry Melchior Muhlenberg by John Wollaston 1760." However, more questions than answers are raised by these inscriptions. First, the name of the woman is erroneous as it was Anna Maria Weiser who married Henry Melchior Muhlenberg; Anna Eve Weiser was her mother. Second, the portraits do not compare favorably with known works by John Wollaston. Third, the sitters do not appear to be a Lutheran minister and his wife based on their clothing, which stylistically dates to about 1730 rather than 1760. The couple in the portraits also appear to be at least in their fifties or sixties. Anna Maria Weiser was not born until 1727, making it very unlikely that she would have had white hair in 1760 (the date on the plaque). Who, then, are the people in the portraits? One possibility is that they might be Conrad Weiser (1696–1760) and his wife, Anna Eve (c. 1705–81), though the fact that no portraits are listed in the probate inventory of Weiser's estate makes this claim problematic. In addition, the only known portrait painted of Conrad Weiser during his lifetime (see fig. 1.16) depicts him with dark hair and a beard—very different from the clean-shaven man wearing a wig in the portrait in question. Another possibility is that the sitters could be Frederick Muhlenberg's in-laws, David and Maria Catharine Schaeffer, since the portraits descended in his family. Frederick owned "6 Pictures" valued at £6.15 when he died in 1801, which included portraits of himself and his wife by Joseph Wright (see figs. 3.15 and 3.16) and four other examples.

Figs. 4.3 and 4.4. Portraits of unknown man and woman, probably by Jacob Maentel (1778–1863?), Pennsylvania, c. 1815.

From the *Muhlenberg Album*

Although identified as Conrad and Anna Eve Weiser, the clothing of the sitters in these portraits dates them to about 1815. The subjects may be a later Conrad Weiser and his wife. The portrait of the woman was identified in the *Muhlenberg Album* as being "from a sketch found in York, Pa." The portraits relate strongly to the work of Jacob Maentel (1778–1863?), an itinerant artist who painted the portraits of many Pennsylvania German families in the early 1800s.[1]

Fig. 4.5. Portrait of Henry Melchior Muhlenberg (1711–87), probably by Jacob Eichholtz (1776–1842), Lancaster, c. 1815.

From the *Muhlenberg Album*

A copy of this painting is illustrated in fig. 2. That portrait was donated by descendant Alletta Morris McBean to the Preservation Society of Newport County in 1986, along with a copy of Peter Muhlenberg's portrait, as part of the furnishings of her house, Chepstow. The last-known owner of the original portrait, thought to be by Jacob Eichholtz, was Mrs. William E. Chisholm of College Point, Long Island. Born Mary Ann Rogers (1827–1913), she was the daughter of Mary Ann Muhlenberg (Mrs. John Rogers), who was the granddaughter of Frederick Augustus Muhlenberg. The portrait probably descended from Frederick to his son, Henry William Muhlenberg (d. 1805), who was the father of Mary Ann Muhlenberg Rogers. According to the provenance supplied to the Frick Art Reference Library by Mrs. Henry Lawrence Chisholm in 1957, the portrait passed from Mary Ann Muhlenberg Rogers to her daughter, Mary Ann Rogers (Mrs. William E. Chisholm, 1827–1913) of New York, then to her son George E. Chisholm of Morristown, N.J., then in 1937 to his cousin William Garnett Chisholm of New York, then to Henry Lawrence Chisholm of Tuxedo Park, N.Y., then to his widow, Mrs. Henry Lawrence Chisholm (Rosalind Robinson) of Bedford, N.Y.

Fig. 4.6. Portrait of Henry Melchior Muhlenberg (1711–87), after Charles Willson Peale, probably 1800s.

Collection of a descendant

This portrait is one of numerous copies of the original portrait, painted by Charles Willson Peale, which is unlocated. An engraving by James W. Steel, after the original, was published in 1869 (see fig. 3.3). Peale also painted Henry Muhlenberg Jr. in 1810 while Peale was on a visit to Lancaster; that portrait is now in the collection of Independence Hall. Seven years later, Peale attended an exhibition of the American Academy at New York in 1817, where he reported seeing "a picture which I believe had been copied from a portrait I painted of the late Revd. Mr. Muhlenbergh." Most likely he was referring to the portrait of Henry Jr., who had died only two years previous in 1815.[2] The original Peale portrait probably descended from Henry Muhlenberg's widow, Anna Maria, to her daughter Mary Swaine. Mary's husband, Francis Swaine, bequeathed "the portrait of my late father in law the Reverend Doctor Henry Muhlenberg" to his nephew Henry Augustus Muhlenberg in his will of 1820. The portrait then descended to Henry Augustus Muhlenberg's son, Dr. Hiester Henry Muhlenberg (1812–86), then to his son Nicholas H. Muhlenberg (b. 1856), to his brother Charles H. Muhlenberg (b. 1870), to his son Charles H. Muhlenberg Jr. (b. 1899) of Reading, Pa. Its present whereabouts are unknown.

Fig. 4.7. Portrait of Peter Muhlenberg (1746–1807), probably by John Trumbull (1756–1843), c. 1790–1800.

From the *Muhlenberg Album*

Numerous portraits of Peter Muhlenberg, probably based on this painting, are known, including the one illustrated in fig. 2.1. The last-known owner was Mrs. Mary A. Chisholm in 1910.

Fig. 4.8. Silhouette of Anna Barbara Muhlenberg (1751–1806), probably Pennsylvania, c. 1800.

From the *Muhlenberg Album*

This is the only known depiction of Peter Muhlenberg's wife, Anna Barbara or "Hannah" Meyer. The last-known owner was Isaac Hiester in 1909.

Fig. 4.9. Certificate of Peter Muhlenberg's membership in the Society of the Cincinnati, 1785.

American Philosophical Society

This certificate, which is signed by George Washington, documents Peter Muhlenberg's membership in the Society of the Cincinnati. The last-known family member to own it was Major Frank P. Muhlenberg in 1910.

Fig. 4.10. Jug, owned by Peter Muhlenberg, probably Staffordshire or Liverpool, England, c. 1800.

From the *Muhlenberg Album*

According to family history, this jug was given to General Peter Muhlenberg by his officers. The decoration includes a scene of the apotheosis of Washington, based on a print after his death on December 14, 1799, with traces of gilding around the rim. The last-known owner was Major Frank P. Muhlenberg in 1910.

Fig. 4.11. Dinner service, coffeepot, punch bowl, and sugar bowl, owned by Peter and Hannah Muhlenberg, c. 1790–1800.

From the *Muhlenberg Album*

The punch bowl in this photograph is illustrated in figs. 3.19 and 3.20; the last-known owner of the other objects was Dr. William F. Muhlenberg in 1910. The coffeepot and plates appear to be Chinese export porcelain while the sugar bowl appears to be of silver and glass.

Fig. 4.12. Sugar bowl, possibly owned by Peter and Hannah Muhlenberg, by Samuel Richards Jr. (c. 1765–1827), Philadelphia, c. 1803–6.

Diplomatic Reception Rooms, U.S. Department of State, Washington, D.C.

According to family tradition, this silver sugar bowl was owned by General Peter Muhlenberg and his wife, Hannah. The "MM" cipher engraved on it may be a combination of Muhlenberg and Meyer (Hannah's maiden name). Alternatively, the sugar bowl may have been owned by one of Peter's nieces. A silver tablespoon with the initials "M M" engraved in a closely related manner (see fig. 4.60) descended in the family of Maria Salome Muhlenberg Richards and was probably first owned by her daughter Mary Catharine Richards (1785–1866), who married Isaac Myers (1787–1864) of Reading, Pa., in 1816. The "M M" cipher may thus stand for Mary Myers.[3]

Figs. 4.13 and 4.14. Masonic apron and collar, owned by Peter Muhlenberg, probably Philadelphia, c. 1800.

Collection of a descendant

Peter Muhlenberg, along with his brother Frederick and brother-in-law Francis Swaine, was a member of the Free and Accepted Masons. All three joined the Royal Arch Lodge No. 3 in Philadelphia in 1779. The designs embroidered on this silk apron include a sprig of acacia (symbolizing eternal life), star, crescent moon, and sun (containing the letter G within a triangle), with an all-seeing eye on the flap. The purple trim of the apron, along with the velvet collar, may indicate Peter's rank as past master or his affiliation with the Royal Arch degrees.[4]

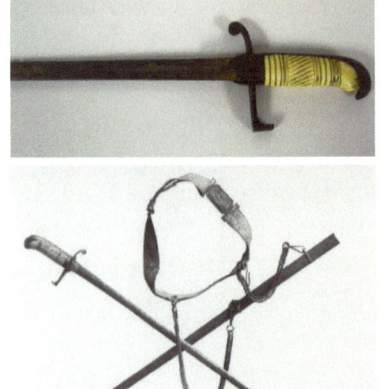

Fig. 4.15. Sword, scabbard, and waist belt, with history of ownership by Peter Muhlenberg, c. 1810–1815.

From the *Muhlenberg Album*

According to family tradition, this sword was owned by General Peter Muhlenberg (1746–1807). Based on the style of the handle, however, it probably dates to the War of 1812 and was more likely owned by one of his sons. It is possible that the blade may date earlier and was rehilted. This sword was sold at Pook & Pook, Downingtown, Pa., September 28-29, 2007, lot 482. The waist belt and another sword that has been associated with General Peter Muhlenberg, but also dates c. 1810–15, remain in the possession of descendants.

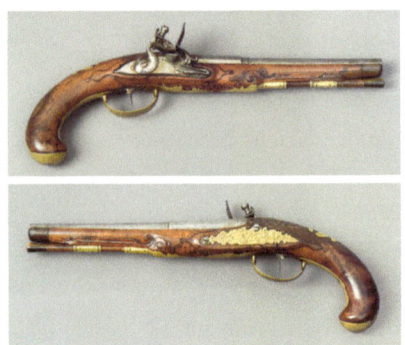

Fig. 4.16. Pistol, owned by Peter Muhlenberg, probably Germany, c. 1740–50.

Collection of Brian and Barbara Hendelson

"P. Muhlenberg" is engraved on the sideplate of the pistol, which may refer to either General Peter Muhlenberg (1746–1807) or his son Peter Jr. (1787–1844).

Fig. 4.17. Photograph of Esther Muhlenberg Hiester (1785–1872), c. 1865.

From the *Muhlenberg Album*

The eldest daughter of General Peter Muhlenberg, Esther married Dr. Isaac Hiester of Reading in 1810.

Fig. 4.18. Portrait miniature of Dr. Isaac Hiester (1785–1855), probably Reading, Berks County, c. 1820–25.

Collection of a descendant

Dr. Isaac Hiester studied medicine at the University of Pennsylvania and practiced in Reading for nearly forty years. He was the first president of the Berks County Medical Society, formed in 1824. The miniature is inscribed on the back "Dr. Isaac Hiester / Taken by Mr. Schamer."

Fig. 4.19. Portrait of Mary Denny (1807–93), c. 1830.

From the *Muhlenberg Album*

Fig. 4.20. Portrait of Francis Swaine Muhlenberg (1795–1832), c. 1825.

Historical Society of Trappe, Collegeville, Perkiomen Valley, Inc.

A son of General Peter Muhlenberg, Francis Swaine Muhlenberg married Mary Denny and became a congressman in Ohio. After his death she married Richard Hopkins. The last-known owner of Mary Denny's portrait and a similar portrait of Francis Swaine Muhlenberg was Mrs. Thomas J. Emery (born Mary Muhlenberg Hopkins) of Cincinnati in 1910.

Fig. 4.21. Portrait of Peter Muhlenberg Jr. (1787–1844), attributed to Jacob B. Schoener (1805–47), probably Reading, Berks County, c. 1840.

Private collection; photo courtesy Pook & Pook

Fig. 4.22. Portrait of Sarah Coleman Muhlenberg (1803–60), c. 1830.

Historical Society of Trappe, Collegeville, Perkiomen Valley, Inc.

Peter Muhlenberg Jr. married Sarah Coleman in 1826 (see fig. 3.30 for another portrait of him).

Fig. 4.23. Tea table, owned by Eve Elisabeth Muhlenberg Schultze (1748–1808), Philadelphia, c. 1766.

From the *Muhlenberg Album*

According to family tradition, this tilt-top tea table was given by General Peter Muhlenberg to his sister, Eve Elisabeth, upon her marriage to Christopher Emanuel Schultze on September 23, 1766. The last-known owner was Mary Janet Vanderslice of Philadelphia in 1910.

Fig. 4.24. Portrait of Susan Kimmel Schultze (1781–1860), Pennsylvania, c. 1810.

From the *Muhlenberg Album*

Susan Kimmel married John Andrew Melchior Schultze (1775–1852), son of Eve Elisabeth Muhlenberg Schultze (see fig. 3.38 for his portrait). The last-known owner of this portrait was Miss A. E. Schultze of Philadelphia in 1910.

Fig. 4.25. Photograph of Maria Magdalena Schultze (1787–1875), c. 1865.

From the *Muhlenberg Album*

The youngest child of Eve Elisabeth Muhlenberg and Christopher Emanuel Schultze, Maria Magdalena married John Cameron.

Fig. 4.26. Sampler, by Maria Magdalena Schultze (1787–1875), Berks County, 1800.

Private collection; photo courtesy of M. Finkel & Daughter

This sampler was worked by the youngest daughter of Eve Elisabeth Muhlenberg and Christopher Emanuel Schultze. In 1785, Henry reported in his journals that "Margreth, the oldest daughter of Mrs. Schultze, took the opportunity to send her grandmother a sample of her skill at sewing as a present." Margreth (Anna Maria Margaretta) was then thirteen years old, the same age as her sister Maria Magdalena when she worked this sampler in 1800.

Fig. 4.27. Portrait of Frederick Augustus Muhlenberg (1750–1801), attributed to Jacob Eichholtz (1776–1842), Lancaster, c. 1838.

The Speaker's House, Trappe, Pa., gift of Sven and Jessica Muhlenberg

This is one of two portraits of Frederick Muhlenberg painted by Eichholtz about 1838 for Muhlenberg descendants, based on the original by Joseph Wright (see fig. 3.15).[5]

Fig. 4.28. Portrait of Mary Catharine Muhlenberg Hiester (1774–1846), attributed to John Neagle (1796–1865), Philadelphia, 1838.

Martin Art Gallery, Muhlenberg College, Allentown, Pa.

The oldest daughter of Speaker Frederick Muhlenberg, Mary Catharine married John S. Hiester of Reading.[6]

Fig. 4.29. Portrait of John S. Hiester (1774–1849), probably by John Neagle (1796–1865), Philadelphia, c. 1838.

From the *Muhlenberg Album*

John Sylvanus Hiester was the son of General Joseph Hiester of Reading. The last-known owner of his portrait was Henry M. Hiester of Mercersburg, Pa., in 1910.

Fig. 4.30. Portrait of Mary Catharine Sheaff Muhlenberg (1778–1851), attributed to Jacob Eichholtz (1776–1842), Lancaster, c. 1835.

From the *Muhlenberg Album*

The daughter of Philadelphia merchant William Sheaff, Mary Catharine married Henry William Muhlenberg (1772–1805), son of Speaker Frederick Muhlenberg. They had three children: William Augustus Muhlenberg (see fig. 3.33), Dr. Frederick Augustus Muhlenberg (see fig. 4.31), and Mary Anne Muhlenberg. Her brother, George Sheaff, married a daughter of Frederick Muhlenberg (see fig. 4.33). The last-known owner of this portrait was Mrs. Richard S. Barrows (Mary Gillis Chisholm) of New Alexandria, Va., in 1966.

Fig. 4.31. Portrait of Dr. Frederick Augustus Muhlenberg (d. 1837), attributed to Jacob Eichholtz, Lancaster, c. 1817 or c. 1837.

From the *Muhlenberg Album*

A grandson of Speaker Frederick Muhlenberg via his son Henry William, Dr. Frederick Augustus Muhlenberg was a physician in Flushing, Long Island, until his death from consumption in 1837. The papers of Jacob Eichholtz include a letter from Dr. William Augustus Muhlenberg in 1837 referencing a portrait by Eichholtz of his brother, Dr. Frederick Augustus Muhlenberg, and asking for it to be improved or a new version made. It may be the portrait Eichholtz painted in 1817 of "Dr. A. Muhlenberg." In 1838 Eichholtz received $100 from W. A. Muhlenberg, but whether he made a new portrait or improved the previous one is unclear. The last-known owner of this portrait was B. Ogden Chisholm, son of Mrs. William E. Chisholm (Mary Ann Rogers), who owned it in 1910.[7]

Fig. 4.32. Portrait of Mary Ann Catharine Muhlenberg Rogers (1798–1879), probably Pennsylvania, c. 1840.

Martin Art Gallery, Muhlenberg College, Allentown, Pa.

Mary Ann Catharine Muhlenberg was the daughter of Henry William Muhlenberg and granddaughter of Speaker Frederick Muhlenberg and Catharine Schaeffer. She married John Rogers of New York.

Fig. 4.33. Portrait of Anna Catharine Muhlenberg Sheaff (1781–1865), probably Pennsylvania, c. 1810.

From the *Muhlenberg Album*

Anna Catharine was the daughter of Speaker Frederick Muhlenberg and Catharine Schaeffer. She married George Sheaff (1779–1851) in 1800 and lived at the Highlands in Fort Washington, Montgomery County, Pa. The last-known owner of this portrait was Mrs. David McMurtie Gregg of Reading, Pa., in 1910.

Fig. 4.34. Portrait miniature of John Peter David Muhlenberg (1785–1849), probably Pennsylvania, c. 1815.

From the *Muhlenberg Album*

The youngest son of Speaker Frederick Muhlenberg and Catharine Schaeffer, David Muhlenberg married Rachel Evans, daughter of famed inventor Oliver Evans, and was a steam engineer. The last-known owner of this portrait was Mrs. David McMurtie Gregg of Reading, Pa., in 1910.

Fig. 4.35. Portrait of Margaretta Henrietta Muhlenberg Kuntze (1751–1831), probably New York, c. 1818.

Historical Society of Trappe, Collegeville, Perkiomen Valley, Inc.

Fig. 4.36. Portrait of John Christopher Kuntze (1744–1807), attributed to John Wesley Jarvis, New York, 1818.

New-York Historical Society, 1818.1

These portraits of Henry and Mary Muhlenberg's second daughter, Margaretta Henrietta, and her husband depict them as an older couple in comparison with the portraits illustrated in figs. 1.37 and 1.38. No owner was listed when those portraits were published in 1910.

Fig. 4.37. Tea service, owned by Margaretta Henrietta Muhlenberg Kuntze and John Christopher Kuntze, probably New York, c. 1795.

From the *Muhlenberg Album*

The last-known owner of this silver tea service was Mrs. Henry O. DuBois of New York in 1910.

Figs. 4.38 and 4.39. Portraits of Catharine Eliza Kuntze (1776–1863) and Caspar Meier (1774–1839), probably New York, c. 1800.

From the *Muhlenberg Album*

Daughter of John Christopher Kuntze and Margaretta Henrietta Muhlenberg, Catharine Eliza Kuntze married Caspar Meier of New York in 1801 and lived at Willow Bank, Bloomingdale, located at the intersection of Riverside Drive and 119th Street. The last-known owner of these portraits was Mrs. Henry O. DuBois of New York in 1910.

Fig. 4.41. Daguerreotype of Catharine Frederica Kuntze (1789–1869), c. 1845.

From the *Muhlenberg Album*

Daughter of John Christopher Kuntze and Margaretta Henrietta Muhlenberg, Catharine Frederica Kuntze married Daniel Oakley (1779–1857) of New York. The last-known owner of this daguerreotype was Mrs. C. H. Morley in 1910.

married Jacob Lorillard of New York in 1809. The last-known owner of this portrait was H. Schuyler Cammann, her great-grandson, who donated it to the New-York Historical Society in 1945.

Fig. 4.43. Portrait of Jacob Lorillard (1774–1836), probably New York, c. 1835.

From the *Muhlenberg Album*

Jacob Lorillard was a merchant in New York. The last-known owner of this portrait was Mrs. Lewis G. Morris of New York in 1910. Later portraits of Lorillard and his wife, Anna Margaretta Kuntze, also exist and are now in the collection of the Preservation Society of Newport County at Chepstow, the former home of their descendant Alletta Morris McBean.

Fig. 4.40. Portrait miniature of Maria Magdalena Kuntze (1785–1838), New York, c. 1815.

From the *Muhlenberg Album*

Daughter of John Christopher Kuntze and Margaretta Henrietta Muhlenberg, Maria Magdalena Kuntze did not marry. The last-known owner of the portrait was Meta Ward of New York in 1910.

Fig. 4.42. Portrait of Anna Margaretta Kuntze (1791–1846), possibly by Samuel Waldo (1783–1861) and William Jewett (1795–1874), New York, c. 1835.

New-York Historical Society, 1945.446

The youngest daughter of John Christopher Kuntze and Margaretta Henrietta Muhlenberg, Anna Margaretta Kuntze

Appendix A

Figs. 4.44 and 4.45. Candlesticks, silver pitcher, and ceramic wares of Henry Muhlenberg Jr. (1753–1815).

From the *Muhlenberg Album*

According to family tradition, these objects were owned by Henry Muhlenberg Jr., youngest son of Henry Melchior and Anna Maria Muhlenberg. The last-known owner was Dr. William F. Muhlenberg of Reading, Pa., in 1910.

Fig. 4.46. Portrait of Henry Augustus Philip Muhlenberg (1782–1844), probably Pennsylvania, c. 1840.

Collection of a descendant

Eldest son of Henry Muhlenberg Jr., Henry Augustus Philip Muhlenberg was the minister of Trinity Lutheran Church in Reading and later a U.S. Congressman. An earlier portrait miniature of him is depicted in fig. 3.36.

Fig. 4.47. Sampler, by Mary Elizabeth Hiester (1784–1806), Reading, Berks County, 1795.

Winterthur Museum purchase with funds provided by the Henry Francis du Pont Collectors Circle, 2009.6

Mary Elizabeth Hiester was the first wife of Henry Augustus Philip Muhlenberg; after her death in 1806 during the delivery of their first child, he married her older sister Rebecca.[8]

Fig. 4.48. Portrait possibly of Rebecca Hiester (1781–1841), probably by William Witman, Reading, Berks County, c. 1795.

Collection of Kurt and Valerie Malmberg

The young woman depicted in this portrait may be Rebecca Hiester, daughter of Joseph Hiester, a Revolutionary War general and governor of Pennsylvania. The sitter holds in her lap a manuscript music book, strikingly similar in appearance to one that was owned by Rebecca Hiester and dated 1791 (now in the collection of the Winterthur Library). Numerous details of the painting, including the green Windsor chair in which the girl is seated and the billowing curtain with tassels in the background, relate closely to a portrait of Reading clockmaker Daniel Rose that was painted by William Witman of Reading about 1795. Witman was probably related to the Hiesters by marriage as Joseph Hiester's wife, Elizabeth, was the daughter of Adam and Catharine Witman of Reading.[9]

Fig. 4.49. Music book of Rebecca Hiester Muhlenberg, Reading, Berks County, 1791.

Winterthur Library, Joseph Downs Collection of Manuscripts and Printed Ephemera

First owned by Rebecca Hiester, this music book then passed to her daughter, Rosa Catharine Muhlenberg.

Fig. 4.50. Portrait miniature of Rosa Catharine Muhlenberg Nicolls (1820–67), probably Pennsylvania, c. 1845.

Private collection; photo courtesy of Pook & Pook

Daughter of Henry Augustus Philip Muhlenberg, Rosa Catharine married Gustavus Anthony Nicolls (1817–86) in 1846. After Rosa's death he married her cousin Ann Hall Muhlenberg, daughter of Dr. Frederick Augustus Muhlenberg of Lancaster.

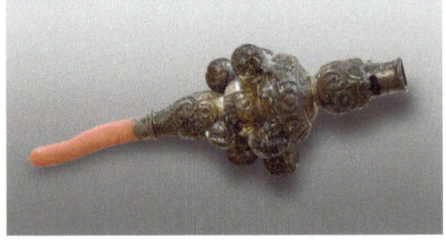

Fig. 4.51. Baby rattle, probably owned by Henry Augustus Muhlenberg (1823–54), by George Unite (1798–1896), Birmingham, England, c. 1825.

Historical Society of Trappe, Collegeville, Perkiomen Valley, Inc.

This silver baby rattle, with whistle tip and coral teething stick, is engraved "H A Muhlenberg," probably in reference to Henry Augustus Philip Muhlenberg's son, Henry Augustus (1823–54). The rattle is marked "GU" for George Unite (act. 1825–96), a prolific silversmith known for making small silver items such as baby rattles, snuff boxes, and inkwells.

Fig. 4.52. Portrait of Dr. Frederick Augustus Hall Muhlenberg (1795–1867), by Jacob Eichholtz (1776–1842), Lancaster, 1813.

LancasterHistory.org, Lancaster, Pa.

Fig. 4.53. Portrait of Eliza Schaum Muhlenberg (1799–1826), by Jacob Eichholtz (1776–1842), Lancaster, c. 1816.

Private collection; photo courtesy of Christopher T. Rebollo Antiques

Son of Henry Muhlenberg Jr., Dr. Frederick Augustus Hall Muhlenberg was a physician in Lancaster. A later portrait of him is depicted in fig. 3.35. He married Eliza Schaum of Lancaster in 1816, which was probably the occasion on which her portrait was painted. Another portrait of Eliza, also painted by Eichholtz, is in the collection of the Pennsylvania Academy of Fine Arts. It is unclear which portrait is the one referred to in Eichholtz's ledger for 1816.[10]

Fig. 4.54. Portrait of Francis Swaine (1754–1820), probably by John Neagle (1796–1865), Philadelphia, c. 1820.

In his will of 1820, Francis Swaine directed his executors to have a copy of his portrait made by Bass Otis of Philadelphia and bequeathed it to his niece, Eliza (Kuntze) Meier (see fig. 4.38). The administrative accounts of Swaine's estate, however, reveal a payment to "John Nagle" of $20 on October 17, 1820, and on July 12, 1821, $11.25 to "Wm Pike for framing a Portrait." No payment to Otis is listed, suggesting that the executors chose to have John Neagle paint the portrait instead.

Fig. 4.55. Pistol, owned by Francis Swaine (1754–1820), probably Lehigh Valley, Pennsylvania, c. 1775.

The Timothy D. Wagner Family Collection

One of a pair, this silver-mounted pistol is engraved "F S" on the thumbpiece for Francis Swaine. It probably dates to his military service during the American Revolution. Swaine was later sheriff of Montgomery County from 1787 to 1790. He probably gave the pistols to his namesake nephew, Francis Swaine Muhlenberg (1795–1832), youngest son of Peter Muhlenberg (see fig. 4.20). In Swaine's will of 1820, he bequeathed to his "beloved nephew" his house in Reading, a gold watch, large silver tankard, and $5,000.

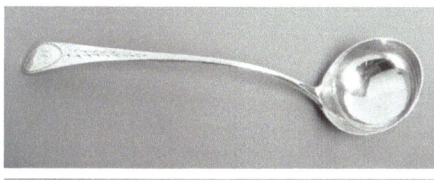
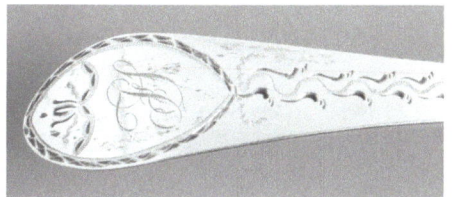

Fig. 4.56. Ladle, owned by Francis Swaine (1754–1820), by Jacob Kucher (act. c. 1802–33), Philadelphia, c. 1800.

Collection of a descendant

Engraved "F S" on the handle, this ladle was first owned by Francis Swaine. After his death, it then probably passed to the family of his sister-in-law, Maria Salome Muhlenberg Richards, as Francis and his wife had no surviving children. It then descended in the Richards family to the present owner.

Fig. 4.57. Card table, owned by Maria Salome Muhlenberg Richards (1766–1827), probably Pennsylvania, c. 1800.

From the *Muhlenberg Album*

According to family tradition, this card table, with inlaid bellflowers on the legs, was owned by Maria Salome Muhlenberg Richards. The last-known owner was Mrs. Henry Melchior Muhlenberg Richards of Lebanon, Pa., in 1910.

Fig. 4.58. Stand, owned by Maria Salome Muhlenberg Richards (1766–1827), Pennsylvania, c. 1800–1810.

Collection of a descendant

This tilt-top stand has a history of ownership by Maria Salome Muhlenberg Richards and was probably made in either Montgomery or Berks Counties.

Fig. 4.59. Teapot, cup, and saucer, owned by Maria Salome Muhlenberg Richards (1766–1827), China, c. 1790–1800.

Collection of a descendant

Made of Chinese export porcelain, this teapot, cup, and saucer have a history of ownership by Maria Salome Muhlenberg Richards.

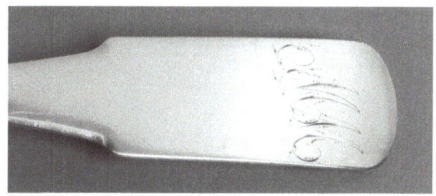

Fig. 4.60. Tablespoon, probably owned by Mary Catharine Richards Myers (1785–1866), by William Mannerback (1762–1838), Reading, Berks County, c. 1816.

Collection of a descendant

The initials "M M" engraved on this tablespoon probably stand for Mary Catharine Richards, eldest daughter of Maria Salome Muhlenberg and Matthias Richards, who married Isaac Myers (1787–1864) of Reading, Pa., in 1816. A similar cipher is engraved on the sugar bowl illustrated in fig. 4.12, which may also have belonged to Mary (Richards) Myers.[11]

Fig. 4.61. Portrait of Matthias Swaine Richards (1787–1862), Pennsylvania, c. 1840.

From the *Muhlenberg Album*

Matthias Swaine Richards was a merchant and surveyor in Reading, Pa. The last-known owner of his portrait was Mrs. Matthias H. Richards in 1910.

Fig. 4.62. Tablespoon and two teaspoons, owned by Elizabeth Salome Richards (1794–1873), by John Tanguy (1780–1858), Philadelphia, c. 1815.

Collection of a descendant

These three silver spoons are engraved "E S R," for Elizabeth Salome Richards, a daughter of Maria Salome Muhlenberg Richards, and bear the mark of John Tanguy, a Philadelphia silversmith active from 1801 to 1822.

Figs. 4.63 and 4.64. Portraits of John William Richards (1803–54) and Andora Garber (1815–92), probably Pennsylvania, c. 1840.

From the *Muhlenberg Album*

The youngest child of Maria Salome Muhlenberg and Matthias Richards, John William Richards married Andora Garber of Trappe, Pa., in 1835. The last-known owner of their portraits was Mrs. Matthias H. Richards in 1910.

Fig. 4.65. Seal of the Muhlenberg family.

Private collection; photo courtesy of Pook & Pook

Engraved on this seal is the Muhlenberg family coat of arms, featuring a rampant lion holding a sword and wheel.

APPENDIX B:
THE FIRST THREE GENERATIONS OF THE MUHLENBERG FAMILY

Henry Melchior Muhlenberg (September 6, 1711–October 7, 1787)
    m. **Anna Maria Weiser** (June 24, 1727–August 23, 1802) on April 22, 1745

1. John Peter Gabriel Muhlenberg (October 1, 1746–October 1, 1807)
    m. Anna Barbara Meyer (February 28, 1751–October 27, 1806) on November 6, 1770
        Daughter (d. 1773)
        Henry Myers Muhlenberg (1775–1806), unm.
        Charles Frederick Muhlenberg (1778–95), unm.
        Esther Muhlenberg (1785–1872), m. Isaac Hiester (1785–1855)
        Peter Muhlenberg Jr. (1787–1844), m. Sarah Coleman (1803–60)
        Mary Anne Muhlenberg (1793–1805)
        Francis Swaine Muhlenberg (1795–1832), m. Mary Denny

2. Eve Elisabeth Muhlenberg (January 29, 1748–July 21, 1808)
    m. Christopher Emanuel Schultze (December 25, 1740–March 11, 1809) on September 23, 1766
        Anna Maria Margretta Schultze (1772–1849), m. Michael Ege (1774–1824)
        Henry Christopher Emanuel Schultze (1774–1824), m. Maria Elisabeth Miller (1775–1843)
        John Andrew Melchior Schultze (1775–1852), m. Susan Immel (1781–1860)
        Frederick Augustus Samuel Schultze (1777–1836), m. Mary Rosina Hiester (1781–1824)
        John Peter Gabriel Schultze (1779–1840), m. Mary Magdalena Immel (1788–1853)
        Catharine Elizabeth Schultze (1781–1815)
        Christiana Salome Schultze (1784–1854), m. John Albright (1780–1847)
        Elizabeth Schultze (1785–1861)
        Mary Magdalena Schultze (1788–1875), m. John Cameron (1797–1841)

3. Frederick Augustus Conrad Muhlenberg (January 1, 1750–June 4, 1801)
    m. Catharine Schaeffer (October 29, 1750–December 3, 1835) on October 15, 1771
        Henry William Muhlenberg (1772–1805), m. Mary Catharine Sheaff (1778–1851)
        Mary Catharine Muhlenberg (1774–1846), m. John Sylvanus Hiester (1774–1849)
        Elisabeth Muhlenberg (b. c. 1776), m. John Mifflin Irwin (d. 1814)
        Margaret Catharine Muhlenberg (1778–1874), m. Jacob Sperry (1773–1830)
        Anna Catharine Muhlenberg (1781–1865), m. George Sheaff (1779–1851)
        Frederick Muhlenberg (1783–99), unm.
        John Peter David Muhlenberg (1784–1849), m. Rachel Evans (1790–1848)

4. Margaretta Henrietta Muhlenberg (September 17, 1751–October 23, 1831)
    m. John Christopher Kuntze (August 5, 1744–July 24, 1807) on July 23, 1771
        Maria Kuntze (b. 1773)
        Maria Catharine Kuntze (b. 1774)
        Catharine Eliza Kuntze (1776–1863), m. Caspar Meier (1774–1839)
        Anna Maria Catharine Kuntze (b. 1778)

Hannah Christina Kuntze (b. 1779)
Charles Henry Kuntze (d. 1808), unm.
Joanna Beata Kuntze (b. 1783)
Maria Magdalena Kuntze (1785–1838), unm.
Catharine Frederica Kuntze (1789–1869), m. Daniel Oakley (1779–1857)
Anna Margaretta Kuntze (1791–1846), m. Jacob Lorillard (1774–1836)

5. Gotthilf Henry Ernst Muhlenberg (November 17, 1753–May 23, 1815)
m. Mary Catharine Hall (December 26, 1756–May 1, 1841) on July 26, 1774
Mary Catharine Muhlenberg (1776–1843), m. John Musser (1774–1813)
Susanna Elizabeth Muhlenberg (1779–1836), m. Peter Schmidt (1780–1831)
Henry Augustus Philip Muhlenberg (1782–1844), m.(1) Mary Elizabeth Hiester
(1784–1806) and m.(2) Rebecca Hiester (1781–1841)
John Philip Emanuel Muhlenberg (1784–1825), m. Susan Ann Craig
Peter Samuel Muhlenberg (1786–1827), unm.
Mary Henrietta Muhlenberg (1789–1850), unm.
Philippa Elizabeth Muhlenberg (1791–1869), m. Henry Huffnagle (1787–1826)
Frederick Augustus Hall Muhlenberg (1795–1867), m.(1) Elizabeth Schaum
(1799–1826) and m.(2) Anna Eliza Duchman (1807–1881)

6. Maria Catharine Muhlenberg (November 4, 1755–October 15, 1812)
m. Francis Swaine (January 2, 1754–June 17, 1820) on August 9, 1775
George Washington Swaine (1779–96)
Maria Margaretta Swaine (1788–92)
Frederick Augustus Muhlenberg Swaine (1791–95)
Anna Maria Swaine (1795–97)

7. John Enoch Samuel Muhlenberg (August 21, 1758–February 16, 1764)

8. John Carl Muhlenberg (November 18, 1760–November 24, 1760)

9. Catharina Salome Muhlenberg (April 18, 1764–August 20, 1765)

10. Maria Salome Muhlenberg (July 13, 1766–March 13, 1827)
m. Matthias Richards (February 26, 1758–August 4, 1839) on May 8, 1782
Henry Muhlenberg Richards (1783–1822), m. Elizabeth Otto (1789–1877)
Mary Catharine Richards (1785–1866), m. Isaac Myers (1787–1864)
Matthias Swaine Richards (1787–May 11, 1862), m. Margaret Myers (1785–1858)
Margaret Henrietta Richards (1789–1861), unm.
John Christopher Richards (1791–91)
Charles Richards (1792–1823)
Elizabeth Salome Richards (1794–1873), m. James Farmer McElroy (1787–1839)
Charlotte Francisca Richards (1802–67), m. George Oakley (1807–74)
John William Richards (1803–54), m. Andora Garber (1815–92)

11. Emanuel Samuel Muhlenburg (July 11, 1769–December 24, 1769)

ENDNOTES

Introduction

pp. 1-5

1. Much of the biographical information in this study is derived from the extensive writings of Henry Melchior Muhlenberg, including Theodore G. Tappert and John W. Doberstein, trans. and eds., *The Journals of Henry Melchior Muhlenberg*, 3 vols. (1942; reprint, Camden, Maine: Picton Press, 1980); Kurt Aland, ed., *Die Korrespondenz Heinrich Melchior Mühlenbergs: Aus der Anfangszeit des Deutschen Luthertums in Nordamerika*, 5 vols. (Berlin: Walter de Gruyter, 1986–2002); and John W. Kleiner and Helmut T. Lehmann, trans. and eds., *The Correspondence of Heinrich Melchior Mühlenberg*, vols. 1-2 (Camden, Maine: Picton Press, 1993–97); and Wolfgang Splitter and Timothy J. Wengert, trans. and eds., vols. 3-4 (Camden, Maine: Picton Press, 2009–10). Additional biographical information may be found in William Julius Mann, *The Life and Times of Henry Melchior Muhlenberg* (Philadelphia: G. W. Frederick, 1888); Paul A. W. Wallace, *The Muhlenbergs of Pennsylvania* (Philadelphia: University of Pennsylvania Press, 1950); and Leonard R. Riforgiato, *Missionary of Moderation: Henry Melchior Muhlenberg and the Lutheran Church in English America* (Lewisburg, Pa.: Bucknell University Press, 1980).

2. On the Halle orphanage, see Paul Raabe and Thomas Müller-Bahlke, *Das Historische Waisenhaus* (Halle: Franckeschen Stiftungen, 2005).

Chapter One: Pastors

pp. 7-33

1. Jonathan Dickinson to John Askew, October 24, 1717; cited in Patrick Griffin, *The People with No Name: Ireland's Ulster Scots, America's Scots-Irish, and the Creation of a British Atlantic World, 1689-1764* (Princeton: Princeton University Press, 2001), 101.

2. Theodore G. Tappert and John W. Doberstein, trans. and eds., *The Journals of Henry Melchior Muhlenberg*, 3 vols. (1942; reprint, Camden, Maine: Picton Press, 1980); 2:649–50.

3. On Muhlenberg's experience during the early years of settlement, see Marianne S. Wokeck, "The Desert is Vast and the Sheep are Dispersed: Muhlenberg's Views of the Immigrant Church," in *Henry Melchior Muhlenberg: The Roots of 250 Years of Organized Lutheranism in North America*, ed. John W. Kleiner, Studies in Religion and Society Series, vol. 41 (Lewiston, N.Y.: Edwin Mellen Press, 1998), 85–110.

4. Carl Theo. Eben, trans., *Gottlieb Mittelberger's Journey to Pennsylvania in the Year 1750 and Return to Germany in the Year 1754* (Philadelphia: John Jos. McVey, 1898), 63.

5. John W. Kleiner and Helmut T. Lehmann, trans. and eds., *The Correspondence of Heinrich Melchior Mühlenberg*, vols. 1-2 (Camden, Maine: Picton Press, 1993–97), 1:49; Tappert and Doberstein, *Journals*, 1:67.

6. On the founding of the New Hanover Lutheran congregation and building of churches, see Charles H. Glatfelter, *Pastors and People: German and Lutheran Reformed Churches in the Pennsylvania Field: 1717-1793*, Publications of the Pennsylvania German Society, vol. 13 (Breinigsville, Pa.: Pennsylvania German Society, 1980), 375–76; also Rev. J. J. Kline, *A History of the Lutheran Church in New Hanover, Pennsylvania* (n.p., 1910).

7. On November 13, 1780, after the funeral of Christian Schrack, Muhlenberg noted that the Schracks immigrated in 1717 and settled in Providence, where they "built themselves a makeshift hut and dug a cave beside it, in which they did their cooking, and then established a small shop and inn for travelers." He continued, "When an English inhabitant stayed too long in the cave, came home late, and had a row with his wife, he made excuses and said that he had been in the Trap. From that time on the section was called Trapp, and is known all over America" (Tappert and Doberstein, *Journals*, 3:370; 1:70). On the Moravians in Pennsylvania, see Craig D. Atwood, *Community of the Cross: Moravian Piety in Colonial Bethlehem* (University Park: Pennsylvania State University Press, 2004). On the meeting between Zinzendorf and Muhlenberg, see Walter H. Wagner, *The Zinzendorf-Muhlenberg Encounter: A Controversy in Search of Understanding* (Bethlehem, Pa.: Moravian Historical Society, 2002).

8. Tappert and Doberstein, *Journals*, 2:200.

9. Ibid., 1:84–85; see also Glatfelter, *Pastors and People*, 379–81.

10. The 1750 schoolhouse was replaced in 1793 with a stone one that was razed in 1851. Drawings of the weather vanes appear in Albert H. Sonn, *Early American Wrought Iron*, 3 vols. (New York: Charles Scribner's Sons, 1928), 3:88–89, pl. 245; they also appear in one of the earliest known depictions of the church, in Sherman Day, *A Copious Selection of the Most Interesting Facts, Traditions, Biographical Sketches, Anecdotes, Etc. Relating to Its History and Antiquities, Both General and Local, with Topographical Descriptions of Every County and All the Larger Towns in the State* (Philadelphia: George W. Gorton, 1843). These are among the earliest – known extant American weather vanes. Other known examples, also of wrought iron, include one dated 1699 from a mill on the Chester Creek owned by William Penn, Samuel Carpenter, and Caleb Pusey (see Jack L. Lindsey, *Worldly Goods: The Arts of Early Pennsylvania* [Philadelphia: Philadelphia Museum of Art, 1999], 26); one dated 1710 from a mill in Pennsylvania (sold at Pennypacker Auction Centre, Reading, Pa., *Pennsylvania Dutch Folk Art: The Oustanding Collection of Lamb's Mill*, Kutztown, Pa., September 11–12, 1972, lot 404), and one dated 1753 and attributed to Michael Schaeffer of Rockland Township, Berks County (see Beatrice B. Garvan and Charles F. Hummel, *The Pennsylvania Germans: A Celebration of Their Arts, 1683–1850* [Philadelphia: Philadelphia Museum of Art, 1982], pl. 43).

11. Rev. Charles F. Dapp, *History of Zion's or Old Organ Church* (Spring City, Pa.: Inter-Borough Press, 1919), 14, 133. On Pennsylvania German church pewter, see Donald M. Herr, *Pewter in Pennsylvania German Churches*, Publications of the Pennsylvania German Society, vol. 29 (Birdsboro, Pa.: Pennsylvania German Society, 1995). A similar flagon marked by Alberti is illustrated on p. 89. The Augustus service is not included in this book because it had been stolen; it was later recovered. In addition to the objects illustrated, the service includes two deep plates (bearing the mark of Ann Carter, Southampton, London, act. 1730–54) and two shallow plates (bearing mark of John Townsend and Thomas Compton, London, act. 1785–1801). The New Hanover Lutheran Church also owns an unmarked pewter communion chalice of English or Continental origin in addition to an English-made pewter tankard and large dish; see Herr, *Pewter*, 49–50, 76, 106, 177.

12. Raymond J. Brunner, *That Ingenious Business: Pennsylvania German Organ Builders*, Publications of the Pennsylvania German Society, vol. 24 (Birdsboro, Pa.: Pennsylvania German Society, 1990), 64–65. Some authors have confused the Trappe organ with one made by Johann Adam Schmahl of Heilbronn, Germany, which was installed at St. Michael's in 1751. The New Hanover organ was built by Christian Dieffenbach (1769–1829) of Bethel Township, Berks County; see Brunner, *Ingenious Business*, 116–17.

13. Tappert and Doberstein, *Journals*, 1:91, 117.

14. Glatfelter, *Pastors and People*, 23, 50–52, 55–58, 74–75, 119–20, 125–26; see also Charles H. Glatfelter, *The Pennsylvania Germans: A Brief Account of their Influence on Pennsylvania*, Pennsylvania History Studies, no. 20 (University Park: Pennsylvania Historical Association, 1990), 16–17.

15. Tappert and Doberstein, *Journals*, 3:36; see also Glatfelter, *Pastors and People*, 411–20.

16. Adolph B. Benson, *Peter Kalm's Travels in North America*, vol. 1 (New York: Wilson-Erickson, 1937), 21.

17. Gottlieb Mittelberger claimed that he transported the Schmahl organ when he immigrated in 1750, but Brunner shows that this claim is doubtful, based on the account of the organ by Pastor Peter Brunnholtz in 1752; see Brunner, *Ingenious Business*, 49–54.

18. Tappert and Doberstein, *Journals*, 2:277.

19. A second pewter communion flagon attributed to the "Love" maker of Philadelphia, dating c. 1775–1800, was later acquired by St. Michael's; see Herr, *Pewter*, 99.

20. Tappert and Doberstein, *Journals*, 1:210–11.

21. Ibid., 1:94, 102.

22. Paul Wallace, *Conrad Weiser: Friend of Colonist and Mohawk* (Philadelphia: University of Pennsylvania Press, 1945). On the Weiser and Muhlenberg genealogies, see Frederick S. Weiser, ed., *Weiser Families in America*, 2 vols. (New Oxford, Pa.: John Conrad Weiser Family Association, 1997). A painting in the collection of the Philadelphia Museum of Art (acc. no. 69-284-13) is said to depict Weiser but probably dates to the 1800s; for an illustration, see Beatrice B. Garvan, *The Pennsylvania German Collection* (1982; reprint, Philadelphia: Philadelphia Museum of Art, 1999), 337.

23. Tappert and Doberstein, *Journals*, 1:102–4.

24. Inventory of Conrad Weiser, taken July 30–31, 1760, Berks County Courthouse, Reading, Pa.

25. Tappert and Doberstein, *Journals*, 1:71, 118. None of these early houses survive; two log dwellings were described by Thomas Schwenk in 1899, based on his boyhood recollections of Trappe from the 1810s. One was "an old one-story log house with the chimney on the outside at one of the gable ends." The other was an "exact twin" with the chimney "built up along the outside at the gable end" (see "Recollections of Col. Thomas Swenk, Octogenarian," in *The Perkiomen Region* 2, no. 2 [May 15, 1899]: 24–26; reprinted in William T. Parsons, ed., *History Sketches of Trappe and Collegeville, 1812–1912* [Collegeville, Pa.: Chestnut Books, 1990], 11–12).

26. For a more extended discussion of the architecture of the house, see Lisa M. Minardi, "Of Massive Stones and Durable Materials: Architecture and Community in Eighteenth-Century Trappe, Pennsylvania" (Master's thesis, University of Delaware, 2006), 14–44. Tappert and Doberstein, *Journals*, 1:104. The 1769 description is from a sheriff's sale notice placed in *The Pennsylvania Gazette*, March 2, 1769. In 1763 the Muhlenbergs had sold the property to Friedrich Martins, but he defaulted on the payments. Consequently, it was put up for sheriff's sale and bought by Lorenz Hipple of Chester County, who in 1772 sold it to George Diehl, an elder at Augustus Lutheran church. Diehl sold the property in 1783 to Nicholas Schwenk, who transferred it in 1785 to his son Jacob, a tanner.

27. Mark Oldenburg, "The 1748 Liturgy and the 1786 Hymnal," in Kleiner, *Henry Melchior Muhlenberg*, 61–68.

28. Tappert and Doberstein, *Journals*, 1:245, 441–42.

29. Kleiner and Lehmann, *Correspondence*, 1:316; Tappert and Doberstein, *Journals*, 1:118, 234, 261, 577.

30. Tappert and Doberstein, *Journals*, 1:261, 274, 280, 339, 346.

31. Ibid., 1:467, 590, 627–28; 2:35, 277. Six chairs from the set are known to be extant, along with three chairs that were made c. 1850 in Lancaster. In addition to the illustrated pair, one is in the collection of the Historical Society of Berks County, and three are in a private collection. The illustrated pair descended in the Muhlenberg family and were last sold at Pook & Pook, Downingtown, Pa., *Charming Forge Mansion: The Collection of Earle and Yvonne Henderson*, October 1, 2010, lot 99. Five chairs from the original set and the three later examples were sold at Pennypacker Auction Centre, Reading, Pa., *Collections from the Estates of Minnie T. Nicolls and Frederick W. Nicolls Jr.*, June 25–26, 1962, lots 525, 526.

32. Tappert and Doberstein, *Journals*, 2:29–32, 34–35.

33. Ibid., 2:221.

34. Glatfelter, *Pastors and People*, 411–16, 420. Tappert and Doberstein, *Journals*, 3:454. Charles R. Peterson, *Robert Smith: Architect, Builder, Patriot, 1722–1777* (Philadelphia: Athenaeum of Philadelphia, 2000), 89–93. Brunner, *Ingenious Business*, 85–87. S. Robert Teitelman, *Birch's Views of Philadelphia: A Reduced Facsimile of the City of Philadelphia . . . as it Appeared in the Year 1800* (1982; reprint, Philadelphia: University of Pennsylvania Press, 1983), pls. 6–7, 11.

35. Tappert and Doberstein, *Journals*, 1:248, 261–63, 498; 3:337. After Muhlenberg's death, demand for the introduction of more frequent English-language services grew, particularly in the Philadelphia congregation. In 1804 Peter Muhlenberg led a group that advocated for English services, in opposition to the senior pastor, Justus Heinrich Christian Helmuth. This debate led to the founding of St. John's Lutheran Church in 1807, and by the fall of 1815, a bitter controversy between the two factions finally resulted in legal action the following year; see Friederike Baer, *The Trial of Frederick Eberle: Language, Patriotism, and Citizenship in Philadelphia's German Community, 1790 to 1830* (New York: New York University, 2008); see also Steven M. Nolt, *Foreigners in Their Own Land: Pennsylvania Germans in the Early Republic*, Publications of the Pennsylvania German Society, vol. 35 (University Park: Pennsylvania State University Press, 2002).

36. Tappert and Doberstein, *Journals*, 2:222, 268, 298–99, 404.

37. Ibid., 1:394, 398, 508–9, 595, 667; 2:1, 159, 418, 468, 534–35, 545–46, 638, 713; 3:673, 681.

38. Ibid., 1:190, 332–33, 571; 3:442, 543, 615; see also Renate Wilson, *Pious Traders in Medicine: A German Pharmaceutical Network in Eighteenth-Century North America* (University Park: Pennsylvania State University Press, 2000); Muhlenberg's letter regarding his wife's sale of medications is cited on p. 145.

39. Tappert and Doberstein, *Journals*, 1:623; 2:318, 3:340. On Peter's experience in Germany, see William Germann, "The Crisis in the Early Life of General Peter Muhlenberg," *Pennsylvania Magazine of History and Biography* 37 (1913): 298–329.

40. Cited in Wolfgang Splitter, *Pastors, People, Politics: German Lutherans in Pennsylvania, 1740–1790* (Trier, Germany: Wissenschaftlicher, 1998), 199.

41. Glatfelter, *Pastors and People*, 93–98. On Woodstock, see Joseph B. Clower Jr., ed., *Yesterday in Woodstock according to Fred Painter* (1981; reprint, Woodstock, Va.: Woodstock Museum of Shenandoah County, 1997).

42. Tappert and Doberstein, *Journals*, 2:514, 525, 775.

43. Rayner Wickersham Kelsey, ed., *Cazenove Journal 1794: A Record of the Journey of Theophile Cazenove through New Jersey and Pennsylvania (Translated from the French)* (Haverford: Pennsylvania History Press, 1922), 73; on the church and statues, see Mary Catherine Lee Wood, "Statuary at the Evangelical Lutheran Church of the Holy Trinity in Lancaster, Pennsylvania: Matthew, Mark, Luke, John and a Community with a Mission (Master's thesis, University of Delaware, 2007).

44. Inventory of Emanuel Schultze, taken April 11, 1809, Tulpehocken Township, Berks County, Berks County Courthouse. Glatfelter, *Pastors and People*, 74–75, 125–26.

45. These portraits descended in the family of Mary Muhlenberg Swaine's sister, Maria Salome Muhlenberg Richards.

46. Tappert and Doberstein, *Journals*, 3:519, 522. Henry Muhlenberg to John Swaine, April 19, 1783, in Kurt Aland, ed., *Die Korrespondenz Heinrich Melchior Mühlenbergs: Aus der Anfangszeit des Deutschen Luthertums in Nordamerika*, 5 vols. (Berlin: Walter de Gruyter, 1986–2002), 5:527.

47. Two years after Mary's death in 1812, Francis Swaine married widow Elizabeth Arndt (1764–c. 1831) of Easton. She was the daughter of Zacharias and Christina Margaretha Nyce of Montgomery County and in 1782 married Jacob Arndt Jr., who died in 1812. After marrying, the Swaines lived in Norristown until 1817, when they moved to Reading. On January 8, 1817, Francis advertised the property in Norristown for sale, describing the house as "32 feet six inches in front, 38 feet deep, with two commodious Parlours, large Hall and eight Chambers, piazza between the back Parlour and Kitchen, with Cellars under the whole. The house has been recently repaired, painted, and papered. The lot is 75 feet front by 250 feet deep, with an excellent garden, a good barn, carriage-house, milk-house, &c." See Judith A. H. Meier, *Advertisements and Notices of Interest from Norristown, Pennsylvania, Newspapers*, vol. 1, *1799–1821* (Apollo, Pa.: Closson Press, 1987), 103. After Swaine's death in 1820, Elizabeth married William Ambrose Lloyd; see John Stover Arndt and Warren Smedley Ely, *The Story of the Arndts* (Philadelphia: Christopher Sower Co., 1922), 168.

48. Tappert and Doberstein, *Journals*, 3:486.

Chapter Two: Patriots

pp. 35–47

1. Theodore G. Tappert and John W. Doberstein, trans. and eds., *The Journals of Henry Melchior Muhlenberg*, 3 vols. (1942; reprint, Camden, Maine: Picton Press, 1980); 2:712–15. Anna Maria Muhlenberg to Eve Elisabeth Schultze, April 11, 1775; microfilm, American Philosophical Society.

2. Tappert and Doberstein, *Journals*, 2:34, 35, 77, 713; 3:213. Jacob Schrack returned to Trappe in May, but his illness resurfaced and he was again placed in the hospital, where he died in 1777.

3. Ibid., 2:713, 715, 718, 721. On the Pennsylvania German experience during the war, see Don Yoder, "The Pennsylvania Germans and the American Revolution," *Pennsylvania Folklife* 25, no. 3 (spring 1976): 2–17; also John B. Frantz, "Religion, the American Revolution, and the Pennsylvania Germans," *Der Reggeboge: Journal of the Pennsylvania German Society* 39, nos. 1–2 (2005): 3–21.

4. Tappert and Doberstein, *Journals*, 2:758, 763, 770; 3:1, 29, 37, 114, 301. For a detailed account of the renovations to the main house and descriptions of the two additions, see Minardi, "Of Massive Stones and Durable Materials," 45–78; see also Nancy Kettering Frye, "Trusting in Providence: Henry Melchior Muhlenberg, the Year 1776," *Der Reggeboge: Journal of the Pennsylvania German Society* 36, no. 2 (2002): 3–24.

5. Theodore G. Tappert, "Henry Melchior Muhlenberg and the American Revolution," *Church History* 11 (1942): 301.

6. Tappert and Doberstein, *Journals*, 2:190–91, 273; 3:76, 103, 157, 624.

7. Cited in Wolfgang Splitter, *Pastors, People, Politics: German Lutherans in Pennsylvania, 1740–1790* (Trier, Germany: Wissenschaftlicher, 1998), 189.

8. Tappert and Doberstein, *Journals*, 3:195–96.

9. Cited in Splitter, *Pastors, People, Politics*, 192.

10. Tappert and Doberstein, *Journals*, 3:2, 454, 534.

11. According to Linda Baumgarten, textile curator at Colonial Williamsburg, the robe is made of silk and wool and dates to the late 1700s, with some later alterations. James Thacher, *A Military Journal during the American Revolutionary War* (Boston: Cottons & Bar-

nard, 1827), 151–52. On the robe legend, see Henry A. Muhlenberg, *The Life of Major-General Peter Muhlenberg of the Revolutionary Army* (Philadelphia: Carey and Hart, 1849); Edward W. Hocker, *The Fighting Parson of the American Revolution: A Biography of General Peter Muhlenberg* (Philadelphia: by the author, 1936); and Joseph B. Clower Jr., *Early Woodstock Facts and Photographs* (Woodstock, Va.: Woodstock Museum of Shenandoah County, 1996), 11–13.

12. The flag was described in 1848 by Henry Augustus Muhlenberg: "The regimental colour of this corps is still in the writer's possession. It is made of plain salmon-coloured silk, with a broad fringe of the same, having a simple white scroll in the centre, upon which are inscribed the words, 'VIII Virga Regt.' The spear head is brass, considerably ornamented. The banner bears the traces of warm service and is probably the only Revolutionary flag still in existence." (Muhlenberg, *Life of Major-General Peter Muhlenberg*, 338–39).

13. Tappert and Doberstein, *Journals*: 1:699. Quotes from Frederick to Peter Muhlenberg are cited in Splitter, *Pastors, People, Politics*, 200–201.

14. Tappert and Doberstein, *Journals*, 3:71, 74–80, 125.

15. Ibid., 3:112, 125, 133, 155. Frantz, "Religion," 10.

16. Tappert and Doberstein, *Journals*, 3:62, 71–74, 78–81, 84, 109, 115.

17. Ibid., 3:198–99, 216.

18. Ibid., 3:479–80, 3:568–69, 593, 632, 688, 699. On the house and store, see Minardi, "Of Massive Stones and Durable Materials," 79–112; also Lisa Minardi, "The Speaker's House: Home of Frederick Muhlenberg," *Der Reggeboge: Journal of the Pennsylvania German Society* 43, no. 1 (2009): 3–19. Frederick Augustus Muhlenberg to Henry Ernst Muhlenberg, Philadelphia, May 15, 1782, American Philosophical Society. On trade, see Thomas M. Doerflinger, *A Vigorous Spirit of Enterprise: Merchants and Economic Development in Revolutionary Philadelphia* (Chapel Hill: University of North Carolina Press, 1986).

19. Information on Peter Muhlenberg's military activity is derived from Muhlenberg, *Life of Major-General Peter Muhlenberg*, supported by his personal correspondence and extant orderly books; see "Orderly Book of Gen. John Peter Gabriel Muhlenberg, March 26–December 20, 1777," *Pennsylvania Magazine of History and Biography* 33–35 (1909–11): 257–78, 454–74; 21–41, 166–89, 336–60, 438–77; 59–89, 156–87, 290–303. On the stolen pistols, see *Valley Forge Orderly Book of General George Weedon* (New York: Dodd, 1902), 69. The pistols descended in the Muhlenberg family until they were discovered in a soup tureen sold in the estate sale of a descendant at Pennypacker Auction Centre, Reading, Pa., *Collections from the Estates of Minnie T. Nicolls and Frederick W. Nicolls Jr.*, June 25–26, 1962.

20. Although the Proctor-Muhlenberg pistols were bequeathed by Peter to his son Henry, Henry died in 1806 without issue and the pistols were probably acquired by Peter Jr. along with the brass-barreled pair. Peter Jr.'s son, Francis Peter Muhlenberg, served during the Civil War and had a daughter, Catharine A. Muhlenberg (b. 1867), who married Frederick W. Franklin of Michigan in 1888. It was probably from this branch of the family that the pistols were acquired by collector Lou Brooks of Marshall, Michigan, who sold them to Avis and Rockwell Gardiner in 1943; the Gardiners later sold them to Tom Seymour of Fort Worth, Texas. They are pictured in *The Magazine Antiques* 101 (February 1972): 392–93; see also Tom Seymour, "The Muhlenberg-Proctor Flintlock Pistols: A Brace of Silver-Mounted Revolutionary War Pistols and Their Owners," *The Gun Report* (July 1972): 40–42. Proctor was a carpenter by trade and is said to have helped build City Tavern in Philadelphia. He was high sheriff of Philadelphia from 1783 to 1786 and later rejoined the military; in 1793 he became a brigadier general of the Pennsylvania militia, later helping to suppress the Whiskey Rebellion, and in 1796 was made major general of the Philadelphia militia. At his death in 1806, the inventory conducted includes "1 Pr. Epaulets and Sword" but no firearms. On Proctor, see Benjamin M. Nead, "A Sketch of General Thomas Proctor," *Pennsylvania Magazine of History and Biography* 4, no. 4 (1880): 454–69; Henry Simpson, *The Lives of Eminent Philadelphians, Now Deceased* (Philadelphia: William Brotherhead, 1859), 822.

21. Morrow and Welsh were gunsmiths who supplied firearms to the Philadelphia Committee of Safety during the Revolution. It is also possible that the Proctor-Muhlenberg pistols date slightly later; an exact date of manufacture is difficult to determine with certainty, but the pistols exhibit several advancements in flintlock technology that were coming into use at the start of the American Revolution, including double-roller frizzen springs to help reduce friction and improve speed and a u-shape ridge on the frizzen to help seal the pan and keep moisture from dampening the gunpowder. In the March 9, 1775, issue of the *New-*

York Journal; or, General Advertiser, gunsmith Gilbert Forbes advertised for sale "double swivel and double roller gun locks," indicating that this technology was present in America prior to the Revolution. The pistols also have mounts for a detachable shoulder stock, now missing, to convert them for use as a carbine or short-barreled rifle. This information is based on Alan D. Gutchess, "Technical & Historical Analysis of a Pair of Silver-Mounted Pistols Marked 'Morrow & Welsh'" (unpub. ms., 2009).

22. Cited in Muhlenberg, *Life of Major-General Peter Muhlenberg*, 427–28.

23. Cited in Splitter, *Pastors, People, Politics*, 200.

24. Tappert and Doberstein, *Journals*, 3:374–76, 525, 560–61, 570.

25. Ibid., 3:650.

Chapter Three: Patriarchs
pp. 49-71

1. Theodore G. Tappert and John W. Doberstein, trans. and eds., *The Journals of Henry Melchior Muhlenberg*, 3 vols. (1942; reprint, Camden, Maine: Picton Press, 1980), 3:111, 143, 178–79, 263–64, 472, 741. Letter of Anna Maria Muhlenberg to Eve Elisabeth Schultze, April 22 [1782], microfilm American Philosophical Society.

2. Tappert and Doberstein, *Journals*, 2:594, 603, 626, 645–46; 3:47, 221, 311, 338. Letter of Anna Maria Muhlenberg to Eve Elisabeth Schultze, March 26, 1779, microfilm American Philosophical Society.

3. Tappert and Doberstein, *Journals*, 3:396, 398, 400, 418, 512, 548, 677.

4. Ibid., 3:596–97.

5. According to the provenance supplied to the Frick Art Reference Library by Charles H. Muhlenberg Jr. in 1962, the Peale portrait passed from Hiester Henry Muhlenberg (1812–86) to his son Nicholas Hunter Muhlenberg (b. 1856), to his brother Charles Henry Muhlenberg (b. 1870), to his son Charles Henry Muhlenberg Jr. (b. 1899). An engraving of the Peale portrait was made by James W. Steel of Philadelphia; a copy owned by Dr. Hiester H. Muhlenberg of Reading, Pa., is illustrated in William B. Sprague, *Annals of the American Pulpit; or Commemorative Notices of Distinguished American Clergymen of Various Denominations*, vol. 9 (New York: Robert Carter & Brothers, 1869), frontispiece. (see fig. 3.3)

6. According to the prvenance supplied to the Frick Art Reference Library by Mrs. Isaac Hiester in 1938, the miniature were owned by Peter Muhlenberg's daughter, Esther Muhlenberg (Mrs. Isaac Hiester), then her son William Muhlenberg Hiester, to his son Isaac Hiester, then to his son William Muhlenberg Hiester.

7. Henry records that Mary was severely scalded on her "left hand, breast, shoulder, right arm, neck, and half of her face" (Tappert and Doberstein, *Journals*, 3:396).

8. Ibid., 3:563, 565, 592, 705, 729–30; see also Mark Oldenburg, "The 1748 Liturgy and the 1786 Hymnal," in *Henry Melchior Muhlenberg: The Roots of 250 Years of Organized Lutheranism in North America*, ed. John W. Kleiner, Studies in Religion and Society Series, vol. 41 (Lewiston, N.Y.: Edwin Mellen Press, 1998), 68–75.

9. Tappert and Doberstein, *Journals*, 3:690, 730–39, 745, 747.

10. Ibid., 2:451, 456; 3:280, 572, 746.

11. Ibid., 3:744.

12. Henry Melchior Muhlenberg to Henry Ernst Muhlenberg, July 29, 1784; Kurt Aland, ed., *Die Korrespondenz Heinrich Melchior Mühlenbergs: Aus der Anfangszeit des Deutschen Luthertums in Nordamerika*, 5 vols. (Berlin: Walter de Gruyter, 1986–2002), 5:689–90.

13. Tappert and Doberstein, *Journals*, 3:371–72, 644.

14. Henry Melchior Muhlenberg to Henry Ernst Muhlenberg, July 11, 1780; Aland, *Korrespondenz*, 5:327.

15. Tappert and Doberstein, *Journals*, 3:596–97, 738, 741, 747, 750–51.

16. Andy McConnell, *The Decanter: An Illustrated History of Glass from 1650* (Woodbridge, England: Antique Collectors' Club, 2004), 208–14.

17. Tappert and Doberstein, *Journals*, 1:590; 2:350, 377, 459, 490–91, 507, 556, 754; 3:118, 164, 190, 222, 279, 301, 375, 380, 444, 464, 512, 583, 585, 667, 678, 750.

18. Cited in Margaret C. S. Christman, *The First Federal Congress, 1789–1791* (Washington, D. C.: Smithsonian Institution Press for the National Portrait Gallery and the U.S. Congress, 1989), 31, 219–21.

19. Kenneth R. Bowling and Helen E. Veit, eds., *The Diary of William Maclay and Other Notes on Senate Debates, March 4, 1789–March 3, 1791* (Baltimore, Md.: Johns Hopkins University Press, 1988), 8, 33, 43, 60, 75, 84, 141, 203, 224, 238, 252, 258, 278.

20. Several modified copies of this portrait are known, including one by Jacob Eichholtz that descended in the family and is now owned by the Speaker's House in Trappe, Pa. (see fig. 4.27), and another by Samuel Bell Waugh (1814–85) that now hangs in the House wing of the U.S. Capitol. On the Wright portraits, see Monroe H. Fabian, *Joseph Wright: American Artist, 1756–1793* (Washington, D. C.: Smithsonian Institution Press for the National Portrait Gallery, 1985), 128–31; also Monroe H. Fabian, "Joseph Wright's Portrait of Frederick Muhlenberg," *The Magazine Antiques* 97, no. 2 (February 1970): 256–57. The settees survive and are now in the Governor's Room of New York City Hall; for an illustration see *The Magazine Antiques* 33, no. 5 (May 1938): 250.

21. Cited in Christman, *First Federal Congress*, 221.

22. A similar chair can be seen in a portrait of Rosina (Hager) Hiester, wife of U.S. Representative Daniel Hiester (1747–1804) from Pennsylvania. This portrait is thought to have been painted by Wright and is now in the collection of the Washington County Museum of Fine Arts; for an image see Jean Woods, *The Germanic Heritage* (Hagerstown, Md.: Washington County Museum of Fine Arts, 1983), 37. When published by Monroe Fabian in his work on Joseph Wright, the portrait of Catharine Schaeffer Muhlenberg was thought to have been lost in a house fire in 1917.

23. Jacob Cox Parsons, ed., *Extracts from the Diary of Jacob Hiltzheimer of Philadelphia, 1765–1798* (1893; reprint, Philadelphia: Kessinger Publishing, n.d.), 227.

24. William Duane to Thomas Jefferson, June 10, 1801, "Letters of William Duane," *Proceedings of the Massachusetts Historical Society*, 2nd ser., vol. 20 (1907): 291.

25. *Poulson's American Daily Advertiser*, October 15, 1807.

26. S. Robert Teitelman, Patricia A. Halfpenny, and Ronald W. Fuchs II, *Success to America: Creamware for the American Market, featuring the S. Robert Teitelman Collection at Winterthur* (Woodbridge, England: Antique Collectors' Club, 2010), 84–85.

27. Other silver associated with Peter Muhlenberg includes an urn-shaped sugar bowl made by Samuel Richards Jr. of Philadelphia that bears the initials "MM"; see fig. 4.12 and also Clement E. Conger, *Treasures of State: Fine and Decorative Arts in the Diplomatic Reception Rooms of the U.S. Department of State* (New York: Harry N. Abrams, 1991), 354.

28. Tappert and Doberstein, *Journals*, 3:146. Eichholtz painted at least five portraits of Henry Muhlenberg Jr.; this one is signed and dated 1811 and was made for Muhlenberg's daughter Mary Catharine (Mrs. John Musser) and descended in the family. See Rebecca J. Beal, *Jacob Eichholtz, 1776–1842: Portrait Painter of Pennsylvania* (Philadelphia: Historical Society of Pennsylvania, 1969), 175–77; also Thomas R. Ryan, ed., *The Worlds of Jacob Eichholtz: Portrait Painter of the Early Republic* (Lancaster, Pa.: Lancaster County Historical Society, 2003), 105.

29. On Henry Muhlenberg Jr., see Paul A. W. Wallace, "Henry Ernst Muhlenberg," *Proceedings of the American Philosophical Society* 92 (May 1948): 107–110; Herbert H. Beck, "Henry E. Muhlenberg, Botanist," *Papers Read before the Lancaster County Historical Society* 32 (1928), 99–107; and J. M. Masch, *Gotthilf Heinrich Ernst Mühlenberg als Botaniker* (New York, 1886).

30. On the Bartram-Muhlenberg correspondence, see Thomas Hallock and Nancy E. Hoffmann, eds., *William Bartram, In Search of Nature's Design: Selected Art, Letters, and Unpublished Writings* (Athens: University of Georgia Press, 2010), 381-425.

31. This sugar bowl was sold at Pennypacker Auction Centre, Reading, Pa., *Collections from the Estates of Minnie T. Nicolls and Frederick W. Nicolls Jr.*, June 25–26, 1962, lot 504, together with a silver tankard, also dated 1774, by Joseph and Nathaniel Richardson.

32. Anne Ayres, *The Life and Work of William Augustus Muhlenberg* (New York: T. Whittaker, 1889); Alvin W. Skardon, *William Augustus Muhlenberg: Church Leader in the Cities* (Philadelphia: University of Pennsylvania Press, 1971). Several portraits of William Augustus Muhlenberg were made by Eichholtz; one is owned by St. Luke Hospital in New York City. See Beal, *Jacob Eichholtz*, 177–178.

33. Two portraits of John Andrew Schultze were made by Eichholtz; see Beal, *Jacob Eichholtz*, 220. On John W. Richards and extracts from his diary, see Margaret H. Hoover, "Trappe, 1834–1836," *Der Reggeboge: Journal of the Pennsylvania German Society* 7 (April 1973): 1–16. Richards married Andora Garber (1815–92) of Trappe.

34. Cited in Stephen Hess, *America's Political Dynasties* (New York: Doubleday & Co., 1966).

Appendix A

pp. 73-84

1. Another portrait, identified as Conrad Weiser III, is pictured in John Joseph Stoudt, *Early Pennsylvania Arts and Crafts* (New York: A. S. Barnes and Co., 1964), 188. On Jacob Maentel, see Mary Black, *Simplicity, A Grace: Jacob Maentel in Indiana* (Evansville, Ind.: Evansville Museum of Arts & Science, 1989); Mary Lou Robson Fleming, "Folk Artist Jacob Maentel of Pennsylvania and Indiana," *Pennsylvania Folklife* 37 (spring 1988): 98-111; and Mary Lou Fleming and Marianne Ruch, "Jacob Maentel: A Second Look," *Pennsylvania Folklife* 41 (autumn 1991): 2-19.

2. Charles Coleman Sellers, *Portraits and Miniatures by Charles Willson Peale* (Philadelphia: American Philosophical Society, 1952), 150. Sellers claimed that Peale was referring to his portrait of Henry Melchior Muhlenberg, but it is equally possible he was referring to the one of Henry Muhlenberg Jr.

3. This sugar bowl is published in Clement E. Conger, *Treasures of State: Fine and Decorative Arts in the Diplomatic Reception Rooms of the U.S. Department of State* (New York: Harry N. Abrams, 1991), 354.

4. On Masonic aprons, see Barbara Franco, *Bespangled, Painted & Embroidered: Decorated Masonic Aprons in America, 1790-1850* (Lexington, Mass.: Museum of Our National Heritage, 1980).

5. Rebecca J. Beal, *Jacob Eichholtz, 1776-1842: Portrait Painter of Pennsylvania* (Philadelphia: Historical Society of Pennsylvania, 1969), 173-74.

6. On Neagle, see *Exhibition of Portraits by John Neagle* (Philadelphia: Pennsylvania Academy of the Fine Arts, 1925).

7. Beal, *Jacob Eichholtz*, 172-73.

8. The Mary Elizabeth Hiester sampler was sold at Pook & Pook, Downingtown, Pa., February 6, 2009, lot 260. On Berks County needlework, see Kathryn Lesieur, "Here in This Garden: Schoolgirl Samplers of Berks County," *Historical Review of Berks County* 71 (spring 2006): 69-77.

9. The Rose portrait is signed "Witman Pinxit;" for an image, see Beatrice B. Garvan and Charles F. Hummel, *The Pennsylvania Germans: A Celebration of Their Arts, 1683-1850* (Philadelphia: Philadelphia Museum of Art, 1982), 156 and pl. 115.

10. Beal, *Jacob Eichholtz*, 174-75, 214. See also Thomas R. Ryan, ed., *The Worlds of Jacob Eichholtz: Portrait Painter of the Early Republic* (Lancaster, Pa.: Lancaster County Historical Society, 2003), 110.

11. On the Mannerbacks, see Terry Royal West and Polly Allison du Pont, *The Mannerbacks: Reading's Master Silversmiths, 1785 to 1870* (Reading, Pa.: Reading Eagle Press, 2010).

ABOUT THE AUTHOR

LISA MINARDI is the leading historian of the Muhlenbergs and their material culture. A graduate of Ursinus College and the Winterthur Program in Early American Culture, she wrote both her undergraduate and master's theses on the Muhlenberg family. She is also president of the Speaker's House, the home of Frederick Muhlenberg, where she is overseeing research and restoration efforts.

A specialist in Pennsylvania German decorative arts, she has catalogued several major fraktur collections, including the Free Library of Philadelphia. She is the coauthor of *Paint, Pattern & People: Furniture of Southeastern Pennsylvania, 1725–1850* and the assistant curator of the accompanying exhibition at Winterthur Museum.

Der Reggeboge

Journal of the Pennsylvania German Society

Volume 45 **2011** Number 1

Editor
Thomas J. Gerhart

Deitsch Editors
Earl C. Haag
C. Richard Beam

Copy Editor
Carolyn C. Wenger

Editorial Consultants
Rev. Larry M. Neff
Dr. Scott T. Swank
Alan G. Keyser
Richard H. Shaner
Annette Kunselman Burgert
Dr. Richard E. Wentz

The Pennsylvania German Society Board of Directors

President
N. Daniel Schwalm
Shamokin, Pa.

Vice president
Rev. Wallace J. Bieber
Whitehall, Pa.

Treasurer
Robert M. Kline, M.D.
Newmanstown, Pa.

Secretary
Carolyn C. Wenger
Ephrata, Pa.

Rev. Wallace J. Bieber
Whitehall, Pa.

Thomas J. Gerhart
Greencastle, Pa.

Norman C. Hoffman
Barto, Pa.

Robert M. Kline, M.D.
Newmanstown, Pa.

Lois F. McClintock
Doylestown, Pa.

N. Daniel Schwalm
Shamokin, Pa.

Ronald S. Treichler
East Greenville, Pa.

Carolyn C. Wenger
Ephrata, Pa.

The Pennsylvania German Society

P.O. Box 244 • Kutztown, PA 19530-0244
Phone: (717) 597-7940 • *E-mail:* pgs@innernet.net • *Web site:* www.pgs.org

Der Reggeboge is published biannually by the Pennsylvania German Society.

Members of the Pennsylvania German Society receive *Es Elbedritsch, Der Reggeboge,* and an annual volume.

Membership Fees

Life (one-time payment per person)	$2,000	once
Benefactor	$650	per year
Sponsor	$325	per year
Sustaining	$125	per year
Couples (one set)	$75	per year
Patron	$65	per year
Associate (no annual volume)	$35	per year
Institutions (libraries, schools, etc.)	$90	per year

International Membership

International Patron	$125	per year
International Institution	$125	per year

The Pennsylvania German Society

P.O. Box 244
Kutztown, PA 19530

Phone: (717) 597-7940
E-mail: pgs@innernet.net
Web site: www.pgs.org

Der Reggeboge publishes scholarly papers and reports concerning all aspects of Pennsylvania German life, culture, and history. Scholarly submissions should follow the *Chicago Manual of Style* and be made digitally although written and typed material will be considered. We also publish materials in Pennsilfaanisch Deitsch (Buffington-Barba orthography preferred) although we encourage writers using other spelling systems to submit their material as well. For information about all submissions, e-mail the editor, pgs@innernet.net,
or write:

Editor
The Pennsylvania German Society
P.O. Box 244
Kutztown, PA 19530

www.ingramcontent.com/pod-product-compliance
Lightning Source LLC
Chambersburg PA
CBHW040905020526
44114CB00037B/64